Elements in Austrian Economics
edited by
Peter Boettke
George Mason University

PUBLIC DEBT AS A FORM OF PUBLIC FINANCE

*Overcoming a Category Mistake
and its Vices*

Richard E. Wagner
George Mason University, Virginia

CAMBRIDGE
UNIVERSITY PRESS

University Printing House, Cambridge CB2 8BS, United Kingdom

One Liberty Plaza, 20th Floor, New York, NY 10006, USA

477 Williamstown Road, Port Melbourne, VIC 3207, Australia

314–321, 3rd Floor, Plot 3, Splendor Forum, Jasola District Centre, New Delhi – 110025, India

79 Anson Road, #06–04/06, Singapore 079906

Cambridge University Press is part of the University of Cambridge.

It furthers the University's mission by disseminating knowledge in the pursuit of education, learning, and research at the highest international levels of excellence.

www.cambridge.org
Information on this title: www.cambridge.org/9781108735896
DOI: 10.1017/9781108696050

First published 2019

A catalogue record for this publication is available from the British Library.

ISBN 978-1-108-73589-6 Paperback
ISSN 2399-651X (online)
ISSN 2514-3867 (print)

Public Debt as a Form of Public Finance

Overcoming a Category Mistake and its Vices

Elements in Austrian Economics

DOI: 10.1017/9781108696050
First published online: March 2019

Richard E. Wagner
George Mason University

Abstract: Economists commit a category mistake when they treat democratic governments as indebted. Monarchs can be indebted, as can individuals. In contrast, democracies can't truly be indebted. They are financial intermediaries that form a bridge between what are often willing borrowers and forced lenders. The language of public debt is an ideological language that promotes politically expressed desires and is not a scientific language that clarifies the practice of public finance. Economists have gone astray by assuming that a government is just another person whose impulses toward prudent action will restrict recourse to public debt and induce rational political action.

Keywords: public debt, pricing government, coordination failures, contract as promise, debt default

JEL classifications: B31, D72, E62, H63, P16

ISBNs: 9781108735896 (PB), 9781108696050 (OC)
ISSNs: 2399-651X (online), 2514-3867 (print)

Contents

Economists make a category mistake when they treat democratic govern-ments as indebted. A category mistake arises when qualities are assigned to an entity that that entity cannot logically have. Observation of a traffic jam will show it to move backward (Resnick 1994). It would be a category mistake to treat a traffic jam as a gigantic car that moves backward. To the contrary, a traffic jam is an entity that is distinct from the individual cars that constitute the jam. A traffic jam is an emergent entity that supervenes on the cars that constitute the jam, and the traffic jam has different properties from the individual cars that constitute the jam. For instance, the center of the traffic jam moves backwards as time elapses, even though all cars caught in the jam always move forward. Public debt is similarly distinct from personal debt. Indebtedness describes a relationship between two acting entities. Both individuals and monarchs can be indebted to other entities within a society. Democracies, however, cannot be indebted to other entities within the society. There is no entity within that society from which a democratic legislature borrows. To the contrary, democracies are financial intermedi-aries that bring together people, some willingly and others forcibly. On the one hand, there are people who seek legislative support for programs they favor; on the other hand, there are people who have the means to support those programs but who often would rather not do so and live with lower tax burdens instead. To speak of democratic indebtedness is to employ an ideological language to promote politically expressed desires; such speech is not a scientific language that clarifies the practice of indebtedness within a theory of public finance.

Without doubt, budget deficits and the accumulation of public debt have become commonplace within the world of democratic political economy. When a nation's public debt is divided by the number of its residents, many people will find that their per capita share of public debt exceeds their personal debt. In a now forgotten past, economists often talked of retiring public debt and governments often created what were called "sinking funds" to facilitate this retirement. No longer does one hear talk of estab-lishing sinking funds to help in retiring public debt. All the talk in the early twenty-first century is about "managing" public debt, with such talk reflect-ing a presumption that public debt is likely to grow in perpetuity. In this respect, the Maastricht Treaty, which established the European Union in 1991, expressly treated public debt as something to be kept within "man-ageable" limits. Those limits were expressed by asserting that accumulated public debt in member nations should not exceed 60 percent of GDP, nor should a budget deficit exceed 3 percent of GDP in any single year. Yet in the preponderance of EU nations public debt exceeds 60 percent of GDP.

To be sure, no EU nation currently has a budget deficit that exceeds 3 percent of GDP, though several of them are close and most of them do have budget deficits. It seems clear that deficits and debt are normal features of public finance within the EU nations.

It's the same throughout the United States. Among the 50 states, 49 of them have constitutional requirements that they operate with balanced budgets. Yet the preponderance of those states have budget deficits, and most of those deficits exceed the Maastricht limits. Furthermore, David Primo (2007: 109) explains that in 1978, the American federal government enacted the public law named Byrd-Grassley after its two sponsors in the US Senate. That law prohibited budget deficits after 1981; moreover, that law has never been rescinded, but neither has it instructed fiscal practice. That practice at both state and federal levels embraces budget deficits as part of normal budgetary procedure regardless of statutory or constitutional language.

Lexicographers tell us that the meaning of words is determined by how people use them and not by some authority who says how language should be used. Sure, people occasionally consult dictionaries to check meaning and spelling, so the work of the lexicographers can influence linguistic practice. Still, it is mostly individual usage in practical settings that determines linguistic convention, with lexicographers documenting those conventions. Budgetary practice is similar. Budgetary and political practice display intelligible patterns, so that practice can be described by some set of principles or rules that govern that practice. Those principles that practice reflects, however, may bear little connection to what has been enacted in statutes or in constitutions. Furthermore, those principles change through time even without statutory or constitutional change. The sinking funds that were popular in the eighteenth century, for instance, are no longer used even though sinking funds are neither illegal nor unconstitutional.

It is a category mistake to describe democratic governments as being indebted. Individual legislators can be indebted to other individuals or organizations in their personal accounts, just as the monarchs of old could be indebted to wealthy individuals within the society. Democracies, however, are not truly acting entities. A democracy has no independent source of wealth that it can pledge to creditors. A democracy is just an intermediary organization that manages relationships among individual debtors and creditors. What is described as public debt conceals a complex pattern of promises and obligations among people that have emerged through some political process. To describe democracies as being indebted reflects a confusion of thought that, moreover, corrupts some of the moral foundations of liberal democratic regimes as James Odom (2019) notes in explaining how public debt can contribute to the eroding of principles of justice and public good. This Element examines the confused state of economic theory with respect to public debt. To do this requires an exploration into both the economic theory of public finance and the political philosophy of different forms of government. I start by contrasting the meaning of indebtedness within monarchical and democratic regimes to explain why speaking of democratic governments as being indebted is to commit a category mistake. The rest of the Element probes and amplifies the relevant economic theory and political philosophy, explaining in the process why public debt can undermine the liberal principles that arose when feudal monarchies gave way to liberal republics starting in the eighteenth century, and how the undermining of those principles promoted a new version of the status-based relationships that characterized the old feudalism, which Henry Maine (1861) noted in describing how the replacement of feudal monarchies with liberal republics entailed a shift from status-based relationships to contract-based relationships as a societal default setting. Since the middle of the twentieth century we have been witnessing a resurgence of status-based relationships; growing public indebtedness both reflects and abets that resurgence.

1 Monarchies, Democracies, and Indebtedness

Indebtedness is a relationship between two parties, either persons or organizations, where that relationship fits within the contractual template of promise and obligation (Fried 1981). One party, the debtor, borrows an asset that belongs to the other party, the creditor, and promises to return that asset at some later date in conjunction with supplying the creditor with suitable compensation. What renders that compensation suitable is the creditor's agreement to let the debtor take temporary custody of that asset. Absent duress, a creditor would not give a debtor temporary custody without expecting to receive suitable compensation for granting that custody. To be sure, credit-based relationships do not always work out as the creditor anticipates. The debtor might not return the asset or might return it in damaged condition. Within the private law principles of property and contract, the creditor could pursue a cause of action against the debtor to force the debtor to make good on his promise to the creditor. To have that ability does not guarantee the creditor will be successful in pursuing that action. The debtor might have lost custody of the asset, perhaps because he sold that asset to some unknown buyer and then squandered the proceeds, ending up with no ability to compensate the creditor. Even with a well-working legal system, credit contracts entail some modicum of uncertainty due to events that might transpire in the interval between the initiation of the contract and its conclusion.

The monarchs of old were acting persons, as were the wealthy subjects from whom they sometimes borrowed. Like those subjects, monarchs owned assets and traded on their own accounts. It was a correct use of language to speak of a monarch's indebtedness just as it was accurate to speak of the debt incurred by some of his subjects. Monarchs were enveloped within the same contractual template as were the subjects who lived inside the regime. A significant difference between the monarchical regimes of feudal times and the republican and democratic regimes that replaced them was the abolition of the monarch's personal accounts and their replacement with regime accounts that belonged to no one (Schumpeter 1918). Monarchs owned assets from which they could finance their activities. Indeed, the cameralist writers who arose within the Germanic territories after about 1400 and lasted into the nineteenth century counseled that the princes whom they advised should be able to finance the activities of their regimes by the revenues they could obtain from their forests, mines, and other assets (Tribe 1984; Backhaus and Wagner 1987; Wagner 2012a). Indeed, such cameralists as Justi (1771) claimed that a prince who had to resort to imposing taxes was verging on being a failed prince because well-managed princely property should typically provide princes sufficient revenue to manage their regimes. In this respect, it is notable that around half of state activities within the Germanic lands were financed by prices and fees and not by taxes well into the nineteenth century, in sharp contrast to the public finances to the west where taxation provided more than 90 percent of state revenue (Backhaus and Wagner 1987; Wagner 2012a).

Like an ordinary person, monarchs could sometimes find that their desired expenditures exceeded their liquid assets, and so would seek to borrow to finance those activities. In this desire for loans, a monarch was in the same formal position as an ordinary citizen who sought to borrow from a creditor. As a substantive or practical matter, however, monarchs were not quite like ordinary citizens when it came to credit transactions. Monarchs were instances of what Roger Koppl (2002) calls Big Players. For Koppl, a Big Player is an economic actor who is only incompletely constrained by the ordinary institutional restraints and conventions that govern the market ordering of economic activity. For Koppl, the prime contemporary instances of Big Players are central banks and legislatures. These players are not constrained by ordinary contractual principles. A central bank can create money; it does not have to earn it by supplying services that other people value. It is the same with legislatures, who can make promises to some people without simultaneously imposing liabilities on other people to pay for those promises. While a king incurs obligations to repay creditors just as do ordinary people, the king is not truly an ordinary person. A creditor who did not receive timely payment from an ordinary debtor could take legal action against the debtor. It would not have been so easy to take legal action against a king.

Still, a king operated inside pretty much the same legal framework as did his subjects. In this respect, the signing of Magna Carta in 1215 sought to place the king on the same legal playing field as the other nobles who would have been his creditors in England at that time. A king could not simply appropriate wealth from subjects but had to convince creditors to lend to him. His status as a Big Player gave him some bargaining leverage, but that is all. Furthermore, kings would typically want to maintain goodwill among their creditors to keep open the possibility of future lines of credit. The creditors of an indebted royal sovereign would rationally harbor some concern about being repaid, but that concern was also limited by recognition that kings typically wanted to maintain a good reputation among their creditors, as a literature on sovereign debt explains and as illustrated, for instance, by Bulow and Rogoff (1988, 1989), Calvo (1988), Cruces and Trebesch (2013), Grossman and Van Huyck (1988), and Tomz (2007).

The coming of republican forms of government in the eighteenth and nineteenth centuries abolished the monarchs and their personal accounts. In many cases, monarchs were retained, mostly for purposes of ceremony and remembrance. But no longer were they rulers of their realms. They were effectively put on pension, the size of which was in principle subject to parliamentary discretion. The budgetary powers were transferred to republican parliaments. A parliament, however, was not a person or a family. It did not have dynastic interests in any reasonable sense of the term. Members of parliament did not come to parliament bringing their assets, which they would deploy in their practice of public finance. Their personal assets remained in their private accounts, and they practiced statecraft by collecting taxes in various ways from the population they governed. It is not a category mistake to describe monarchs as being indebted; it is, however, a category mistake to describe democracies as indebted.

Where monarchical regimes could be reasonably described as entrepreneurial states, republican regimes became tax states. This distinction between entrepreneurial states and tax states was set forth by the Austrian economist Rudolf Goldscheid (1917); and Goldscheid's distinction was contested by another Austrian economist, Josef Schumpeter (1918), with Rudolf Hickel (1976) collecting several essays relative to that controversy. The substantive point of issue between Goldscheid and Schumpeter was how to treat the Austrian debt that Vienna had inherited with the end of World War I and the collapse of the Hapsburg regime. The theoretical point of difference between Goldscheid and Schumpeter concerned different orientations for a theory of public finance. Both theorists recognized that republican regimes had replaced feudal monarchies, but they differed in the desirability of different institutional arrangements for governing the republican regimes.

Goldscheid thought that a republican regime that relied on taxation would tend to operate in a manner that eroded wealth or slowed its rate of increase, as compared with the monarchies of old. Goldscheid thought that restoring capital accounts to the new regimes would offset that tendency by leading the new regimes to operate in an entrepreneurial manner in much the same way as private persons operated. In contrast, Schumpeter thought that the new regimes would do poorly in trying to act entrepreneurially, and that a tax state where taxes were relatively low would be superior to transferring significant capital assets to political control. The establishment of capital accounts would not induce parliaments into acting like the monarchs of old. More likely, it would induce those parliaments into consuming capital along the lines that Fritz Machlup (1935) later observed.

A short comparison of the public finance theories of Adam Smith and Johan Gottlob von Justi can be informative both regarding the controversy between Goldscheid and Schumpeter and on the differences between monarchical and republican regimes. Given his premier position within the emergence of classical liberalism, the four maxims of taxation that Adam Smith (1776) advanced in Book V of the *Wealth of Nations* are widely regarded as a scheme for limiting the reach of governmental entities into a society's economic activity. Smith's maxims asserted that

1. Taxes should be levied in proportion to property;
2. Taxes should be certain and not arbitrary;
3. Taxes should be convenient to pay;
4. Taxes should be economical to administer for both taxpayers and state.

Compared with the practice of democratic public finance as it has evolved up to the early twenty-first century, the impact of Smith's maxims in limiting a state's collection of revenue seems reasonably clear, particularly with respect to his first maxim that taxes should be levied at a proportional rate, in contrast to the progressive rates that are common today. Smith's maxim didn't say anything about exemption from tax. A tax that is levied at a proportional rate, but which includes substantial exemption from tax, can be highly progressive. A tax of 10 percent on all income (or property) fits the notion of a proportional tax. In contrast, a proportional tax of 10 percent combined with exemption for the first $50,000 can be highly progressive because the average rate of tax paid increases as income rises beyond $50,000.

Justi (1771, pp. 549–65) also articulated maxims of taxation, though these have not been carried forward in the literature on public finance. Justi's maxims included the same territory as Smith's, but they went beyond Smith in limiting the power to tax. For one of those maxims, Justi asserts that a tax should not deprive a taxpayer of necessary items or cause a reduction in capital. Justi further claimed that a tax should neither harm the welfare of taxpayers nor violate their civil liberties. With respect to maxims of taxation, it would seem reasonable to accord Justi similar status to Smith within the pantheon of liberal public finance (Wagner 2012a).

More significantly, Smith and Justi differed in the proper place of taxation within the practice of public finance. For Smith, taxation was the default setting for public finance. Smith preceded his discussion of taxation by arguing that the state should eliminate its holdings of property, thereby eliminating the revenues they derive from those holdings. In contrast, Justi explained that taxation should be a final or last resort option for public finance. Ideally, a state would not tax at all, and would derive its necessary revenues from the sale of services acquired from the operation of its enterprises. Smith and Justi articulated similar maxims regarding qualities of a desirable system of taxation; however, Smith thought taxation should be the primary instrument of public finance, while Justi thought taxation should be an instrument of last resort.

The different attitudes toward taxation that Smith and Justi expressed are relevant for the distinction between monarchical and democratic public finance, as well as for the controversy between Goldscheid and Schumpeter regarding the possible recapitalization of the state after republics had replaced monarchies. Justi treated the state ideally as a participant within the economic order of a society. The state was one participant among many, all of which operated by the same principles of action and rules of law. In contrast, Smith treated the state as operating outside a society's economic order by intervening into it. Where Smith looked to maxims that would limit the negative features of the state's intervention into society, Justi looked to the establishment of institutional arrangements that would render state activity a generally valued participant within a society's economic arrangements.

One need not take sides with respect to Smith and Justi, or to Schumpeter and Goldscheid, to recognize the significance of political presuppositions for a theory of public finance. The habits of thought economists applied to the feudal monarchies were generally extended to the various forms of democratic and republican regimes that replaced those monarchies. Where there had once stood a king, there now stood a parliament. Other than the morphing of a king into a parliament, nothing of theoretical significance for public finance had changed. The royal sovereign was replaced by a sovereign parliament, with this replacement being without significance for a theory of public finance. In this respect, the noted Swedish economist Knut Wicksell (1896 [1958]) described what he regarded as the sorry state of the theory of public finance at the end of the nineteenth century by lamenting that "the theory of public finance reflects its beginnings when autocracy ruled the west." To counter the prevailing theory, Wicksell sought to articulate some elements of a theory of public finance that would be suitable for democratic regimes.

A monarchy was identified with a person who held the throne, along with the regime having principles of succession for when a monarch dies. Monarchs traded on their own accounts. They had assets that they could use to generate revenue. They had expenses, including the finance of wars. To meet those expenses, they would sometimes borrow from wealthy subjects. All these participants were entangled within a transactional nexus of contract and obligation. Though a monarch was a Big Player inside that nexus, the monarch still needed to maintain that nexus, for its disintegration would probably lead to the regime's disintegration as well.

Habits and conventions of thought that were forged in the presence of monarchical governance were carried over to democratic regimes, as Wicksell recognized in his lamentation. The resulting conceptual error was to equate a parliamentary assembly as formally identical to a monarch despite the obvious descriptive differences between democracies and monarchies. Those descriptive differences were more than matters of mere description; they pointed to deep differences in the operating properties of the different types of regime. The actions of a monarch can be reasonably understood through the economic categories of personal or business choice. The actions of a democratic parliament cannot be so understood, as Wicksell sensed and as the later articulations of the theory of public choice, starting with Kenneth Arrow (1951) and Duncan Black (1958), explained.

Monarchs trade on their own accounts; parliaments do not. Parliaments are forms of financial intermediary, only they operate within an environment where they are largely though not wholly free from competition from other suppliers of similar services. For a national government, a parliament does not face competitive parliaments. It can be different for a federal form of government where a national parliament can face competition from provincial or state parliaments. To be sure, federal governments can also restrict the ability of other governments to compete activities away from the national government, and act instead as entities that cartelize the federal system and which Michael Greve (2012) describes as turning the American constitutional system upside-down by replacing a principle of competition among governments with one of cartelization.

In any case, it is not accurate to describe a democratic parliament as being indebted. The transformation from monarchy to democracy did not transform a monarch into a hydra-headed monarch. Rather, it abolished entirely the position of monarchy, replacing it with a fiscal commons that was managed by a committee whose membership periodically turned over through elections; and Wagner (1992, 2007) and Brubaker (1997) explored public finance from the perspective of a fiscal commons, with Ringa Raudla (2010) amplifying the theory of a fiscal commons. To seek to understand the properties of parliamentary democracy with theoretical concepts and categories fashioned for a monarchy is like trying to understand the properties of a jet aircraft in terms of those of a propeller-driven aircraft. In short, political presuppositions are central to understanding public debt within democratic regimes and for understanding how public debt can corrupt the promise of contract (Wagner 2017b).

2 Political Presuppositions and the Theory of Public Finance

As noted above, the Swedish economist Knut Wicksell (1896 [1958]) lamented what he regarded as the sorry state of the theory of public finance by explaining that

> With some very few exceptions, the whole theory [of public finance] still rests on the now outdated political philosophy of absolutism. The theory seems to have retained the assumptions of its infancy, in the seventeenth and eighteenth centuries, when absolute power ruled almost all Europe ... Even the most recent manuals on the science of public finance frequently leave the impression ... of some sort of philosophy of enlightened and benevolent despotism. (Wicksell 1958: 82)

Wicksell's reference to absolutism and to enlightened and benevolent despotism could have fit in varying degrees the mercantilist and cameralist regimes that had disappeared by the nineteenth century. They did not, however, fit the time when Wicksell was writing, which was a time of democratic republics, and democratic republics are still prevalent today.

Public finance is a theory that pertains to the economic organization of political activity. It is the economic theory of state activity, in contrast to the economic theory of market activity. Wicksell raised the challenge of how to think of the economic organization of state activity within a political context of democratic and republican governments, as against the presupposition that governments were absolutist. The key difference between absolutist and democratic regimes is that with absolutist regimes state activity stems from some ruler's choices and actions. With democratic and republican regimes, by contrast, state activity is not the domain of some ruler but is rather the outcome of some process of interaction among interested participants. The phenomena of public finance in democratic polities emerge from within institutional arrangements that operate through committees and elections (Black 1958) and not through some ruler maximizing his or her utility function.

It is far easier to develop theoretical formulations as if governments are absolutist than it is to recognize them as being democratic. For absolutist regimes, the standard model of choice by consumers or by firms can be used. This setting makes it reasonable to explain state activity as some instance of optimizing choice, which requires only two types of information: an objective function, and a constraint on the ability to maximize that function. A theory of public finance for a democratic polity is vastly more complex because state activity is not reducible to solution of a simple problem in constrained optimization. To the contrary, state activity emerges through interaction among interested participants and, moreover, with that interaction being shaped and constrained by institutional and constitutional rules and principles that speak to the political presuppositions of a theory of public finance. Ringa Raudla (2010) illustrates this point lucidly by explaining the relevance of Elinor Ostrom's (1990) work on the governance of commons settings to public finance, and with Roger Congleton (2011) chronicling the development of parliamentary institutions and practices in the liberal democracies.

To illustrate this point about political presuppositions, I shall compare Wicksell's contemporary Francis Edgeworth (1897) with Wicksell. Edgeworth posed the question of how a ruler should extract the desired volume of revenue from subjects when it is desirable to minimize the utility losses those extractions impose. This question was construed as a simple problem in the calculus of constrained maxima and minima that had entered economics around that time. Edgeworth assumed that subjects received utility from their incomes at a diminishing rate, though they had identical income-utility functions. Within this set of presumptions, despots who were benevolently inclined toward their subjects would extract taxes from the highest incomes where the marginal utility from income was lowest. What resulted was a type of progressive rate schedule where incomes were pared down from the top until the despot had raised the desired amount of revenue.

Edgeworth also recognized that this type of tax schedule would induce people with high incomes to reduce their effort, thereby reducing the income they earn when they are faced with a marginal tax rate of 100 percent. Frank Ramsey (1927) formalized the trade-off between redistributing utilities through taxation and reducing total output, which led later to the creation of a literature on optimal taxation for which James Mirrlees received the Nobel Prize in economics in 1996, and with Mirrlees (1994) providing a survey of his ideas about the concept of optimal taxation. At base, the theory of optimal taxation entails a presumption that public finance is the province of benevolent despots who are construed as seeking to maximize the happiness or welfare of their subjects, using the ability to impose taxes and distribute the proceeds as instruments for maximizing welfare.

This setting for the problem of optimal taxation is equivalent to a despot trying to determine how unequally to slice a pie when the size of the pie shrinks as the pie is sliced with increasing equality. A person may reasonably wonder whether this is a useful approach to taxation for several reasons. One such reason is that the political economy of democratic taxation is far removed from the choices of a benevolent despot. Another reason concerns the possibility that human welfare is not well or usefully approached through tax-and-subsidy programs. My interest here, however, resides not in optimal taxation but in amplifying Wicksell's (1896) lament that the theory of public finance still reflects the political presuppositions of benevolent despotism that were alive when economists began to think about public finance.

The political presupposition of benevolent despotism still has a major presence in the theory of public finance, even if that presence has weakened a bit since James Buchanan (1949) first articulated the contours of a genuinely democratic approach to public finance. That alternative path of theoretical articulation, moreover, animated Buchanan's entire scholarly oeuvre, as Richard Wagner (2017a) explains in his rational reconstruction of Buchanan's oeuvre. Buchanan, like Wicksell a half-century earlier, recognized that the theory of public finance still reflected the political presuppositions of benevolent despotism. For the public finance that Buchanan encountered as a student, the two primary illustrations of benevolently despotic public finance were Edgeworth (1897) and A. C. Pigou (1920, 1928).

Where Edgeworth reasoned in terms of what might be called global or macro public finance in looking to how a state's fiscal activities might influence the aggregate volume of welfare within a society, Pigou operated at a micro level of concern by conceptualizing the state as imposing taxes and subsidies on particular activities within society when those activities were otherwise undertaken without their full costs being taken into account by the people responsible for those activities. Buchanan rejected both forms of normative approach that reflected a presupposition of benevolent despotism and looked instead to approaches that made contract with institutional reality, either as it was encountered or as it might plausibly be constructed. In this respect Buchanan encountered two sources of inspiration, both of which remained with him throughout this career. One was Wicksell. The other was Antonio de Viti de Marco (1936) in English translation, with Buchanan (1960) later coming to acquaint readers with the rich Italianate literature on explanatory public finance that began with Antonio de Viti de Marco (1888). Wicksell and de Viti aside, the literature on public finance that Buchanan encountered as a student treated public finance as being normative in character in that it addressed ideas about the goodness of governmental action within society. These considerable strands of literature comprised what could be called an economics of applied statecraft in that those literatures address problems and situations that legislators and public administrators were imagined to face in discharging their activities within a presupposition that benevolent despotism ruled the democratic lands.

The presumption of benevolent despotism is not so absurd as a superficial or literal consideration of the term might suggest. Such theorists as Edgeworth or Pigou were not so naïve as to think that the public finances were truly operated by benevolent despots. They recognized that the operations of the political world were in the hands of real people (Backhause and Medema 2012; Medema 1996); however, their effective presuppositions about the potential impact of their work on the world of fiscal practice would be determined as if they reflected the judgment of a benevolent despot, a fictional character that Adam Smith invoked in the guise of an impartial spectator. In his biography of John Maynard Keynes, Roy Harrod (1951) explained that Keynes was imbued with what Harrod called the "presuppositions of Harvey Road," Harvey Road being the location of the Keynes family residence in Cambridge. According to Harrod, those presuppositions were that the governance of Great Britain was effectively in the hands of a well-meaning elite who operated through persuasion. This was an elitist and not a democratic theory of public finance, and it belongs to the same theoretical family as older presuppositions of benevolent despotism.

In contrast to the bulk of the literature on public finance, Wicksell and de Viti sought to address public finance from within an explanatory motif that made contact with substantive fiscal practice. Indeed, de Viti served for twenty years as a member of the Italian parliament, in addition to serving as professor of economics at the University of Rome, and with Manuela Mosca (2016) providing a short but lucid overview of de Viti's life and work. Wicksell and de Viti recognized that governments operate inside a society's division of labor. To recognize this position of collective action as occurring inside a social division of labor leads to explanatory questions regarding the standard distinction between market activities and political activities. Many of these explanatory questions are addressed these days under the rubric of the theory of public choice. Starting with Antonio de Viti de Marco (1888), these explanatory questions were also addressed by a creative set of Italian theorists of public finance who sought to set forth an explanatory as distinct from a hortatory or tutelary theory of public finance. To be sure, some of those creative theorists were skeptical about the ability of economic theory to cast useful illumination on political processes, the most notable of whom was Vilfredo Pareto, whose thought Michael McLure (2007) examines.

One of those theorists who sought to place public finance within an explanatory setting was Amilcare Puviani (1903) who wrote *Teoria della illusion finanziaria* [Theory of Fiscal Illusion]. This book has never been translated into English, though James Buchanan (1967) discussed Puviani extensively in chapter 10 of *Public Finance in Democratic Process*. Puviani's book has, however, been translated into German in Puviani (1960). In his foreword to that translation, Gunter Schmölders noted that "over the last century, Italian public finance has had an essentially political science character. The political character of fiscal activity stands always in the foreground .... This work is a typical product of Italian public finance, especially a typical product at the end of the nineteenth century. Above all, it is the science of public finance combined with fiscal politics, in many cases giving a good fit with reality" [my translation].

Two things are worth mentioning about this translation. First, Schmölders was well recognized at the time he sponsored this translation for his work on fiscal psychology, where he sought to inject behavioral and psychological themes into economics far before behavioral economics became a recognized field in economics, as illustrated briefly by Schmölders (1959) and fully by Schmölders (1960). Second, Schmölders's remarks about the political science character of Italian public finance were written well before public choice had become a recognized field of study within economics. For instance, the term "public choice" was created only in 1968, and it was several years later before public choice theorizing attracted serious attention from anything more than a few aficionados. An explanatory orientation toward collective or political activity must first seek to explain or characterize the division of activity within societies as between those activities that are organized through market processes and those that are organized through political processes.

Democracies, unlike monarchies, cannot truly be indebted. For a democratic government operating under prevailing principles of public law, there is no entity in society to which legislators pledge their assets against default on any loan the legislature organizes. Indeed, a democratic legislature does not genuinely receive a loan in the first place. A democratic government can no more be indebted than can a bank. Sure, a bank is obligated to its depositors, who have given the bank temporary custody over their funds. The bank, however, intermediates between those depositors and those who borrow those deposits from the banks. This position as intermediary imposes fiduciary obligations on banks, but it does not render banks indebted entities who have placed their assets at risk in giving temporary custody of those assets to borrowers. To describe democratic governments as indebted is a category mistake because it treats a democratic legislature as if it were a monarch who is trading on his personal account, whereas the legislature is trading across the accounts of individual citizens, to the advantage of some and the disadvantage of others.

The formal principle of a democratic government being an intermediary between two sides of a transaction is identical whatever the size of the relevant government; however, form does not dictate substance. Without doubt, the size of a political entity matters hugely for its operating properties, but this size-related difference does not affect the formal quality of democratic governments as intermediaries. A small town containing a few hundred persons can operate largely informally through obtaining agreement among affected parties. This informal quality is impossible for a city of five million or a nation of 500 million persons. For large-scale polities, parliamentary organization is necessary, and with that organization comes oligarchy and cliques, as Robert Michels (1915 [1962]) explained luminously and which May (1965) reviewed. Bertrand de Jouvenel (1961) provides amplification in remarking pithily on the problem a disinterested parliamentarian would have in fostering open discussion in parliamentary assemblies of even modest size. Discussion allows only one person to speak at a time. It also requires that the speaker have an audience. The larger the political entity, the more severe becomes the organization of parliamentary discussion, eventually resulting in the creation of some parliamentary office to limit access to the agenda. The possessor of that power to limit access to the agenda can influence political outcomes in a manner the possessor supports, giving an oligarchic quality to democratic outcomes along the lines that Michael Levine and Charles Plott (1977) and also Plott and Levine (1978) explained luminously in describing how different political choices could be generated without any underlying change in the preferences of participants, simply by changing the procedures that were used in arriving at some decision.

It is easy enough to understand why economists might have continued to treat public finance as the activity of absolutist regimes even though those regimes had mostly given way to democracies. It is far easier to theorize about some absolute ruler than to theorize about the political activities of democracies. For an absolute ruler, the theoretical task has been treated by economists in their theories of consumption and production. Consumers are treated as maximizers of utility; producers are treated as maximizers of profit. The form of the theory is simple even though application of the theory might require some modicum of subtlety in some instances. For instance, it might appear intuitively obvious that the home delivery of groceries is more expensive in areas where population densities are low than where they are high because drivers must spend more time driving between deliveries, which increases the costliness of providing groceries through home delivery. Suppose, however, that data show the reverse relationship, with the price of home delivery being lower in neighborhoods with low density than in neighborhoods with high density. This observation would not invalidate the theoretical proposition but would rather tell the theorist to dig more deeply into the material. For instance, armed robberies might be more prevalent in the high-density neighborhoods, requiring the business to offer higher wages to attract drivers in those areas.

Shifting attention to issues of public finance, suppose a theorist faces the challenge of explaining the $1 billion or so appropriation the American Congress gives to Amtrak, officially known as the National Railroad Passenger Corporation. It is far simpler analytically to treat this appropriation as the solution to some absolute ruler's maximization problem than to illuminate the transactional network through which this appropriation emerges. Yet this appropriation does emerge as one transaction within a transactional network in which Amtrak is but one entity among many competing for appropriations, as Figure 1, the idea for which was first presented in Wagner (2007: 125–54), illustrates. The left side of Figure 1 describes six politically sponsored enterprises as seeking budgetary appropriations from the legislature. Amtrak is just one among what are really thousands of such enterprises. The right side of Figure 1 shows a small legislature of nine persons, of which two, identified as Primo and Secunda, are partisans of Amtrak. Officials of Amtrak and their legislative partisans take the lead in securing appropriations for Amtrak, and this relationship among officials and partisans provides the institutional setting through which budgets emerge within democratic polities. Among other things, those partisans of Amtrak must reach agreement with some nonpartisans by exchanging support among issues, to secure Amtrak's appropriation. The emergence of budgets within this transactional setting is nothing like the solution of some ruler's maximization problem, and instead is the outcome of some complex process of multisided negotiation where no participant can truly be said to have maximized some objective function even though most of the participants might regard themselves as better off by the action they took. The outcome of the democratic process resembles market outcomes; only the analytical simplicity made possible by private property is absent. Clearly, it is far easier analytically to adopt the fiction of there being a maximizing entity that makes

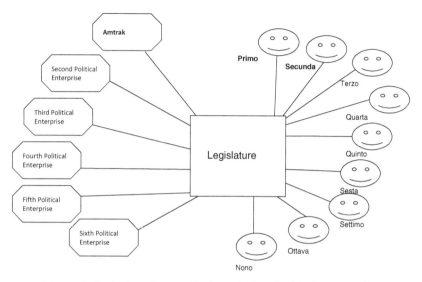

Figure 1 Budgetary intermediation within a legislative assembly

political choices. Such treatment, however, is clearly far-fetched as an explanation of democratic processes, and it is surely analytically superior to try to meet
the challenge of scientific explanation than to evade it by making far-fetched
assumptions.

3 Taxes as Prices: A Useful but Corruptible Simile

Sometimes theorists of public finance describe taxes as "tax-prices" to hold out
the prospect that taxes might serve a similar function to that which prices serve
within a market economy. Taxes are the principal means by which governments
finance their activities. The noted Italian theorist Antonio de Viti de Marco
1936) treated taxes ideally as the fiscal equivalent to market prices, invoking the
term tax-prices (Eusepi and Wagner 2013). It is worth noting that de Viti was
more than a theorist of public finance. Besides serving as Professor of Public
Finance at the University of Rome, de Viti also served for two decades as
a member of the Italian parliament, where he participated in the practice of
public finance. De Viti's treatment of taxes as prices surely entailed some
congruity with the role of prices in a market economy, as it is quite unlikely
that the concepts and categories with which he worked as a member of the
Italian parliament would be divorced entirely from those with which he worked
as a theorist of public finance. In his theoretical work, de Viti advanced two
polar models of a democratic polity. One model was the notion of a cooperative
state, which described a situation where all citizens supported the state's fiscal
activities. The other model was the notion of a monopolistic state where some

citizens were able to use their political dominance to pursue their desires by imposing costs on the remainder of the citizenry. These two models were abstract representations of democratic possibilities. With respect to the substance of political reality, the essays collected in De Viti (1930) revealed de Viti's recognition that monopolistic properties had dominated cooperative properties during what de Viti described as twenty years of struggle. As a general proposition regarding the political organization of collective economic activity, which tendency was dominant within any historical moment would depend on the constitutional and institutional frameworks through which governments were constituted.

To treat taxes as prices is a useful simile for placing the organization of collective economic activity on an explanatory footing. That simile, however, is also easily corruptible because it can easily be treated as a tautology and not a hypothesis. If tax-prices are treated as tautological, governments are construed by assumption as being cooperative states, thereby rendering governments just another form of market participant. By contrast, if the construction is treated as a hypothesis, the tax-price construction can be relevant in some variable degree, with that degree being governed by the constitutional and institutional framework that governs the organization of collective activity. The image of taxes as tax-prices has been known as the benefit principle of public finance, and it reflects the intuitions behind the various contract theories of the state that arose at the end of the Middle Ages. Knut Wicksell (1896), as subsequently adumbrated by Erik Lindahl (1919), set forth a version of this idea that has been carried forward to this day. This analytical framework leads to the effort to place a theory of public finance on the same footing as the theory of a market economy. Whether this can be done or to what extent it might be done is an unsettled matter. For instance, Richard Musgrave (1939) claimed that what he described as the voluntary exchange theory could not be put into practice, meaning that the phenomena of public finance could only be products of arbitrary political authority. Paul Samuelson (1954, 1955) reaffirmed Musgrave's claim in his well-cited papers on the theory of public goods. In contrast, James Buchanan (1967, 1968) sought to explain how the theory of public finance could be placed on an explanatory footing, with his subsequent work on constitutional political economy and philosophy seeking to pursue the problems and opportunities such an effort would have to address to render such a theoretically framework intellectually comprehensible.

Figure 2 illustrates both the opportunities and the difficulties that face any effort to place the social organization of collective activity on an explanatory footing. This figure illustrates a society where aggregate output is divided between public output and private output, as illustrated by R on the production

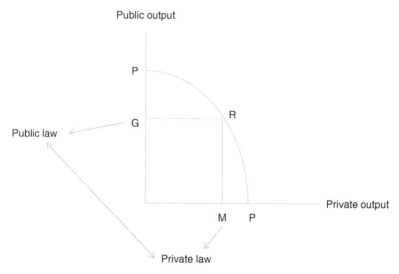

Figure 2 Challenges facing an explanatory theory of public finance

frontier where M denotes a vector of activities organized through market transactions and G denotes a vector of activities organized through political activities. It should be noted that the position denoted by R is *not* an object of choice. Contemporary societies are far too complex for such systemic planning to be possible (Boettke 2001). To the contrary, R denotes two emergent vectors of quantities, both of which emerge through institutionally structured processes that govern interactions among the members of the society. These processes are denoted by the subtended arrows from M and G described as private law and public law. This reference to private and public law lends a greater precision to this formulation than is truly possible. There is little problem with respect to private law because this has been the subject of two centuries of economic theorizing and the economic analysis of law regarding how the private law principles of private property and freedom of contract are able to generate coherent patterns of economic activity.

The conceptual difficulty arises in explaining the political component in Figure 2. No such well-elaborated theory currently exists, though a variety of pieces of such a theory do exist. Indeed, Wagner (2017a) explains that the bulk of James Buchanan's scholarly oeuvre grew out of Buchanan's (1949) statement of the desirability of placing the theory of public finance on an explanatory setting suitable for democratic regimes. One significant obstacle to developing explanatory theories of collective action is the presence of coercion inside democratic regimes, a survey of which is contained among the essays collected in Martinez-Vasquez and Winer (2014). Market organization proceeds through agreement among participants, which means that simple two-person interactions can be treated within the same analytical framework as market interactions involving millions of people; for the rules governing the most complex of interactions are the same as those governing the most elemental of transactions, as Richard Epstein (1995) explains.

When it comes to democratic political economy, coercion will be present in all but small groups where exit from the group is easy. If exit is costly, duress or coercion will often be present. That duress, however, can manifest in numerous ways, which in turn create substantive differences in collective economic activity. This quality of there being an indefinitely large number of paths collective activity can take means that democracy is a generic or formal concept, as opposed to being precise and substantive. Democracy means that political officials secure their positions through competitive election, as opposed to inheriting their positions within monarchies. There are, however, an indefinitely large number of ways that democratic procedures can staff political offices, along with an indefinitely large number of ways that relationships among the holders of democratic offices might be constituted. These considerations grounded in systemic complexity counsel against an effort to develop closed-form models of collective action, as against working with open-ended models.

Further complexity comes about by considering the double arrow that connects private law and public law in the southwest part of Figure 2. This arrow means that the institutional framework denoted as private law is not autonomous from the framework denoted as public law. With respect to their substantive contents, public law and private law are entangled (Wagner 2007, 2016). Private law could correspond to a situation where vendors were free to create whatever contractual terms they chose in their search for profitable business. Within the framework of private law, an attorney and his client might challenge some vendor's contractual stipulations by describing those terms as "unconscionable." The case might be heard before a publicly financed court, and the court's ruling might support the plaintiff, with the precedent thus created leading to changes in commercial contracts because some former commercial practices were ruled unconscionable.

Despite the complexity of the situation, it seems worthwhile to consider briefly Knut Wicksell's (1896) effort to develop an explanatory orientation toward public finance. With respect to Figure 2, Wicksell inquired into the characteristics of a framework of public law, G, inside of which it could be claimed substantively and not just formally that political outcomes reflect the consent of the governed, as Wagner (1988) explains in his examination mostly of the third essay in Wicksell (1896) that was not translated into

English in Wicksell (1958). This recognition must start with understanding that a substantive consent of the governed prohibits situations where people are represented by people against whom they voted. In other words, democratic representation must be a substantive and not just a formal quality. Hence, the system of voting must allow for proportional representation. It also requires that the electoral system provide for a sufficiently large number of parties so that it could reasonably be claimed that the parliament selected through proportional representation could plausibly be construed as a miniature version of Swedish society. To be sure, a skeptic may reasonably doubt that such a miniaturization is possible, but the construction nonetheless illustrates some of the issues that must be faced in developing an explanatory framework for public law that would meaningfully complement the framework of private law.

With parliament as a miniaturization of Swedish society, unanimity within parliament would correspond to unanimity within Sweden, meaning that parliamentary outcomes would reflect the consent of the governed. Wicksell also recognized that unanimity would create tendencies for people to higgle over small matters, thereby impeding the flow of generally beneficial collective activities. In response to this recognition, Wicksell suggested a parliamentary voting rule in the order of five-sixths consent. There is no doubt that Wicksell understated the difficulty in elaborating an institutional framework of public law that would complement the conventional economic framework of private law, but Wicksell's effort illustrates the meaning of the benefit principle of public finance in any case, while also illustrating how this principle seeks to reconcile market pricing and tax financing. Wicksell assumed the presence of a set of procedural principles by which every motion to spend money was accompanied by a placement of liability for the expenditure. Government was conceptualized through the image of contract, with the taxes people agreed to pay being complementary to the market prices they paid. Wicksell's theoretical thinking ran in the direction of constructing political and fiscal arrangements through which the public finances of democratic regimes would have similar properties to market outcomes within an overall scheme of liberal political economy.

4 From Public Pricing to Fiscal Policy: The Keynesian Detour

The 1936 publication of John Maynard Keynes's *General Theory of Employment, Interest, and Money* was a smashing success. The eminent historian of economic theory Mark Blaug (1996: 642) summarizes thusly: "The Keynesian Revolution is one of the most remarkable episodes in the entire history of economic thought; never before had the economics profession been won over so rapidly and so massively to a new economic theory, and nor has it been since." Publication of the *General Theory* was greeted by negative reviews by such eminent economic theorists of the time as Alvin Hansen, Frank Knight, Arthur Pigou, Dennis Robertson, Joseph Schumpeter, Frank Taussig, and Jacob Viner, with Rothschild (1996) surveying the disparate assessments of the *General Theory*. Yet, as Blaug reports, by 1946 "the vast majority of economists throughout the western world were converted to the Keynesian way of think-ing." Indeed, Keynesian thinking was enacted into American legislation with the Employment Act of 1946, which committed the federal government to ensuring full employment through using fiscal policy.

Despite its smashing success, or perhaps because of it, Keynes's *General Theory* also inserted a detour into development of explanatory treatments of public finance. The pre-Keynesian interest that was gaining momentum through a set of Swedish and Italian theorists to set the theory of public finance on an explanatory path of development was cancelled through the unprecedented embrace of fiscal policy as a tool for promoting aggregate economic stability in the aftermath of the Great Depression. While it is perhaps easy to understand the rapt audience that received the message of Keynes's new economics, it is still difficult to understand the widespread embrace of the dubious logic of that new economics. Yet the use of fiscal policy to promote aggregate stability quickly carried the day despite the flimsy logic on which fiscal policy was based.

The orthodox models of fiscal policy that were created after 1936 are easily represented in terms of the income-expenditure theory of aggregate economic theory. That theory held that aggregate income (Y) was equal to aggregate expenditure (E), as described by the relationship $E = C + I + G$. This relationship divides aggregate expenditure into three components: consumption, invest-ment, and government. Aggregate employment, moreover, was claimed to vary directly with aggregate expenditure. The orthodox Keynesian claim on behalf of fiscal policy is that governments can use their budgetary powers to offset volatility in private spending, thereby smoothing that volatility from what it would otherwise have been. While theorists have left behind the simple income-expenditure models that were advanced in the postwar period to explain how fiscal policy could serve as an instrument to promote economic stability, the practice of political economy has remained unchanged despite changes in theoretical formulation. Just look at the various reactions to the economic downturn that started in 2008. The income-expenditure model of the aggregate economy would counsel an increase in government spending to offset the decrease in private spending. The theoretical models used to support that claim were more complex models of stochastic general equilibrium and not the simple arithmetic of C + I + G. Yet the outcome was the same: increase public spending to offset decreases in private spending. How that offset might take place is a policy choice about which options exist. The earlier notions of fiscal policy had governments increasing their real spending. Such more recent notions as quantitative easing had the central bank buying financial assets to promote increased aggregate spending.

There are strong grounds for thinking that the Keynesian creation of fiscal policy to control economic variability entails a detour in the otherwise progressive path of economic theory. The long-standing adherence to the Keynesian idea, moreover, means only that the Keynesian detour has been especially long, but nonetheless represents a detour from the mainline of economic theory (Boettke [2007]). The standard claims on behalf of fiscal policy are incoherent as a first-order proposition, as Robert Barro (1974) explains. According to the income-expenditure framework, an increase in public spending can offset a decrease in private spending, thereby maintaining aggregate spending at its full-employment level. The arithmetic of fiscal policy works well on a classroom whiteboard, but nowhere else. A theorist can go to a whiteboard, postulate an autonomous decrease in I, and then illustrate how an increase in G can offset that fall in I.

Economic life, however, does not proceed in this fashion. For one thing, changes in private spending are not autonomous. They are not the result of sudden and unpredictable changes in animal spirits. Changes in spending result from changes in commercial plans, and these change in response to changes in the expected value people form of different commercial enterprises. The New Deal unleashed a wide variety of new regulatory requirements and regulatory agencies that amounted to creation of a new institutional regime, as Robert Higgs (1997) explains. What might have been a normal pace of recovery from a depression was thus extended through widespread regulation. Higgs's point wasn't that increased spending through fiscal policy flowed into standard commercial channels, but rather was that the New Deal replaced old ways of doing business with new ones, retarding recovery in the process. The New Deal was not an effort to increase G to offset a decrease in I within the income-expenditure theory because it also entailed an effort to transform the American economic system through replacing private ordering with public ordering over wide domains of economic activity. Adaptation to such changes could not have been quick and smooth even in the best of circumstances.

Furthermore, the orthodox claims of fiscal theory are incoherent because they neglect the simple fact that any debt-financed increase in government spending implies an increase in future taxation of equivalent present value to the budget deficit. It is impossible for a government to increase aggregate spending within a society without accounting for other changes that are necessary to accommodate the increase in government spending. This recognition, known as Ricardian equivalence (Barro 1974), means that budget deficits will reduce private spending as people increase their saving to finance the future taxes that a current deficit implies. There is, to be sure, a body of empirical work, surveyed by John Seater (1993), that finds that budget deficits mostly have some positive effect on aggregate spending, though not as much as the pure theory of fiscal policy might suggest. Recognition of these empirical findings raises questions regarding what to make of those findings. One possibility, which points toward the growing interest among economists in behavioral economics, is to assimilate those findings to the presence of fiscal illusion, thereby clashing with the rationality presumed by formulations of Ricardian equivalence.

Within contemporary macro theory, whatever measure is advanced to increase the volume of aggregate spending, it is an increase in public spending that is the antidote to some decrease in private spending, either directly as envisioned by orthodox notions of fiscal policy or indirectly as envisioned by quantitative easing. Either way, aggregate spending is treated as an autonomous variable, in that it determines itself and is not determined by something else. There are other lines of theoretical exposition that recognize that measured spending is not autonomous and uncaused but is, to the contrary, caused by people forming and pursuing commercial and industrial plans. Investment doesn't decline for no reason but declines because investors perceive weakened opportunities for commercial gain. Those weakened opportunities, moreover, can be the aftermath of prior governmental actions that weakened those commercial opportunities. In this situation, increased government spending can intensify rather than smooth volatility, as a considerable literature explains, a few instances of which include Hayek (1932, 1935), Shackle (1968, 1972), Lachmann (1977), O'Driscoll (1977), Witt (1997), Higgs (1997), Garrison (2001), Wagner (2012b, 2012c), Lewis and Wagner (2017), and Veetil and Wagner (2018).

At this point we encounter recognition that standard macro theoretic prescriptions for using governmental policy actions to smooth what is treated as "natural" volatility in private spending is misguided in two significant respects. One respect concerns the theory of the macro or systemic properties of an economic system. Rather than private spending being afflicted by an autonomous waxing and waning of animal spirits, private spending is governed largely by reasoned calculations and projections; however, those projections can be buffeted about by political actions. Hence, policy can be more a source of turbulence than a calmer of turbulence (Wagner 2012c). The second respect concerns the theory of political economy. Orthodox claims on behalf of policy guidance entail a presumption that political actors are fonts of wisdom, with that wisdom being possessed by benevolently self-denying creatures. Neither of these claims is reasonable. Political actors are pretty much like everyone else within the gigantic social division of knowledge that pertains to contemporary life: they know specialized pieces of knowledge directly relevant to their primary activities while being generally ignorant and hence reliant on experts for everything else of significance to them (Koppl 2018). Furthermore, political actors have desires to acquire and use power relative to the preponderance of the population that never seek political office (Schumpeter 1944). In other words, politicians are neither nicer nor wiser than ordinary people, regardless of how they might think of themselves. Indeed, the American constitutional system was founded on exactly this recognition, as Buchanan and Tullock (1962) and Ostrom (1987) explain.

Going forward from here, I shall first review the macro theoretic fallacies that are involved in orthodox claims that governments can use their budgetary powers to smooth variation in private spending, and explain instead how governmental actions are more likely to be sources of volatility than sources for calming volatility. After that, I shall explain the possible conflicts between the working principles of a well-functioning economy and the working principles of democratic arrangements; for over a wide range of territory, those democratic arrangements promote volatility rather than calming it.

5 Ecologies, Not Machines: Analytical Failures of Macro Theories

Much of the imagery of economic theory and economic policy treats economies as mechanisms that sometimes fail as they were designed to perform. This imagery propels economists and their political supporters onto center stage of the human drama because these are the people who claim to have the expertise required to repair the problems encountered and who in turn advise politicians on how to repair the ship of state. This fable of the economist as a mechanic who works in support of the politician-helmsman who sails the ship of state is just that, a fable. It's a piece of mythology. To call this fable a myth is by no means to denigrate myths and their place in our lives. To the contrary, myths offer guidance as we conduct our lives. But some myths offer better guidance than others. Regardless of whether a myth offers good guidance or bad, our resort to myth is an unavoidable feature of the human condition, as can be gleaned from two significant lines of thought from nearly a century ago: Walter Lippman's (1922) book *Public Opinion* and Friedrich Hayek's (1937, 1945) recognition that no person or office in society has possession of all the knowledge that would be necessary to produce the patterns of social life that we experience every day, with Hayek's work explained masterfully by Peter Boettke (2018).

None of us can see the societal entirety, and yet we speak and act as if we can. There is a gap between our sight and our speech, and that gap is bridged by mythology, unavoidably so.

Yet some myths are more informative than other myths. The myth of an economy as a mechanism treats an economy as a machine composed of many parts, any of which can malfunction. The Keynesian theory of fiscal policy and its use of the income-expenditure theory to promote increased government spending as an antidote to any increase in unemployment exemplifies an economy as a machine. The central point behind the myth of mechanism is its presumption that the economic system has been designed by some person or persons who themselves stand apart from the object they have designed. This property of the designer as standing apart from the object that the designer designed provides the template for the orthodox theory of economic policy, including using fiscal policy to control aggregate spending. This image of a designed economic mechanism is surely serviceable in simple societies that entail interaction among a few hundred persons, as illustrated by tribal societies (Schmookler 1984). It is not, however, evenly remotely serviceable for modern complex societies that are ecologies of multitudinous interacting entities, as Roger Koppl (2018) explains in illuminating some implications of that complexity. This ecology is not open to direct control at the systems level because the entities inside that ecology have and pursue their plans of action.

The orthodox theory of economic policy holds that the economic system is mechanical, which means that the pieces inside the system can be repaired in some fashion to perform differently. Hence, the pieces are inert objects to be modified through so-called policy making. Recognition that economies are complex ecologies means that the participants within an economic system choose their preferred courses of action and can modify those courses as they choose. It is impossible for any so-called policy maker to know all the knowledge necessary to modify economic performance with any precision (Boettke 2001). In this respect, we should also remember that a good deal of the relevant knowledge that governs patterns of social interaction is tacit and personal (Polanyi 1958). Polanyi's distinction between tacit and explicit knowledge is significant for thinking clearly about social settings and processes. Explicit knowledge can be reduced to computer code and transferred to other people. Tacit knowledge cannot be so reduced because it pertains to our ability to know something without being able to reduce it to computer code. Tacit knowledge pertains especially to the role of judgment in human action. In part, the operation of a business can be reduced to computer code. That code might instruct a business to stop producing a product after a six-month interval where the firm's system of cost accounting showed the product to be making a negative contribution to the firm's profitability. With this code, the firm would be reduced to mechanism. That mechanism might often give good guidance, as rules of thumb often do.

But it wouldn't invariably give good guidance because computer code ignores tacit knowledge and judgment. Tacit knowledge is genuine knowledge, only it cannot be articulated as through reducing it to computer code. All the same, the use of tacit knowledge is inescapable in economic life. The computer code might say to stop production after six months of losses calculated by the cost accountants. Yet a person on the ground might not be convinced that the computer code is right in this case. The principle of tacit knowledge, moreover, holds that the possessor of that knowledge cannot truly articulate an alternative code that would yield a more accurate judgment. In the presence of tacit knowledge, an economic and social system cannot be reduced to mechanism and computer code. Human judgment by real people in the concrete situations they face is a vital part of societal organization. Recognition of this property of social life raises the question of how to incorporate tacit knowledge into our thinking about economic life when the image of mechanism and its reduction of social life to computer code is inapt.

A reasonable response in this setting is to replace the image of mechanism with one of ecology, as Wagner (2012b) sets forth. With the image of mechanism, the parts perform as their designer intends. Sometimes a defect arises in a part, and the challenge for policy is to locate the malfunctioning part. In simple mechanisms, this will probably be easy. In complex mechanisms with many interacting parts, as illustrated by such massive software code as contained in office suites, it may be difficult to locate points of malfunction, leading the designer to send out patches and updates throughout the life of the program. Still, the parts have all been designed by someone who stands apart from the object that was designed. The code will perform as it was written even if the designer was not aware of some of the interactions that code might have with other parts of complex programs.

In the social world, however, the myriad interacting parts are not designed mechanisms but are people who exist and operate inside the object that the theorist thinks about. Each person has his or her own principles of action, with those principles including tacit as well as explicit knowledge. Once society is envisioned as an ecology constituted as a complex environment of living and interacting parts, and where so-called policy makers are but a subset of those parts, what is described as public policy is no longer captured at all well by the image of a mechanic tinkering with an engine. What is described as an engine by invoking the image of a mechanism is a form of living organism whose myriad parts all pursue their various desires and objectives, and with so-called policy makers doing likewise.

Figure 3 presents a diagrammatic representation of what I have in mind. This diagram separates societies into two levels, a macro level and a micro level. The macro level contains the variables that are the objects of conventional macro theory, as illustrated by the income-expenditure theory. Shown in Figure 3 is the standard representation of a macro economy as denoting equilibrium between aggregate demand and aggregate supply. Within this model, an autonomous increase in government spending within the orthodox model of fiscal policy increases aggregate demand, as illustrated by the shift from AD_1 to AD_2. Barro-like claims on behalf of Ricardian equivalence deny that this increase in aggregate demand is coherent because people will reduce private spending to provide a fund to pay the future taxes that increase in public debt entails. To be sure, much controversy has accompanied claims about Ricardian equivalence, with John Seater (1993) providing a fine summary up to 1993. In short, the predominance of empirical work shows that budget deficits lead to some increase in aggregate spending, only that spending increase is less than it

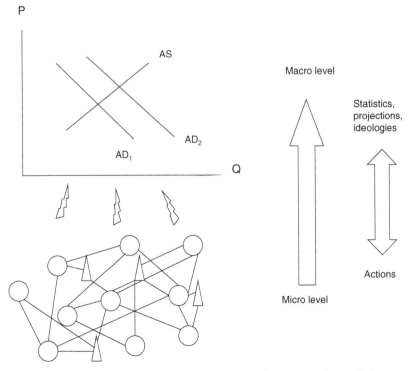

Figure 3 Emergence of aggregate variables within an ecology of plans

would have been if people treated the current tax reductions as wholly equivalent to an increase in their net worth.

At this point it is reasonable to wonder just what such observations might mean. The bottom part of Figure 3 can be useful in this regard. What is described as the macro level is the domain of statistics, projections, and ideologies. It is not the domain of human action in that action can take place only on the micro level. The bottom part of Figure 3 illustrates this distinction between macro and micro levels of an economic system. The lower part of Figure 3 describes an economy as a network of entities, with the circles denoting market-based entities and the triangles denoting political entities. The edges connecting the nodes show patterns of relationship among the entities within the societal ecology. To be sure, Figure 3 displays a terribly simple ecology to illustrate a point, recognizing that actual societal ecologies are so complex that a detailed mapping could not even be drawn. All economic action occurs at the micro level, even actions by governmental entities.

Keeping within the orthodox formulation of fiscal policy, an increase in AD in the upper part of Figure 3 must start by one of the triangles in the lower part receiving authorization to increase its spending. That increased spending, moreover, will spread within the lower part of Figure 3 depending on the types of contractual relationship established among a relevant subset of nodes. How that increased spending projects to the upper level depends on numerous micro theoretic details, which means in turn that there is no unique macro level depiction of the increased spending. For instance, Figure 3 contains ten circles and four triangles, indicating that about 70 percent of economic activity is organized through privately organized enterprises. Alternatively, Figure 3 could have displayed seven circles and seven triangles, indicating equal division of economic activity between privately organized and politically organized enterprises. Furthermore, the increased spending could have been accompanied by a precise assignment to individuals of their future tax liabilities, whereas currently those future liabilities are not assigned in the present. There is good reason for thinking that different methods for determining future liabilities will generate different macro level patterns (Wagner 1986). Stated differently, the aggregative implications of any change in public spending will depend on micro level details of societal interaction. As Roger Garrison (2001) notes pithily, there are many macroeconomic questions, but the answers are all microeconomic in character.

For instance, any projection onto the macro level of Figure 3 must start at some node on the micro level. That node will extend either commercial contracts or regulatory requirements to other nodes, which in turn will influence patterns of economic activity among those other nodes. There is no unique projection that must run from micro to macro because the contexts of interaction matter. Among the circles portrayed in Figure 3, all entities are guided by projections of profitability. All such enterprises speak a common commercial language. When some of those entities are political entities, as are the triangles in Figure 3, a common commercial language of mutual gain gives way to some extent to a political language grounded in duress and obligation, which in turn sets in motion searches by commercial enterprises to escape some of the losses political action might threaten to impose on them. This points toward Higgs's (1997) analysis of how the regime change that began with President Hoover and continued with President Roosevelt impaired what had been normal patterns of economic recovery.

6 Calculation and Coordination within a Political Economy

The economic theory of a market economy presents an explanation of societal coherence when all entities in society relate to one another through the institutional framework of private property and freedom of contract. That theory, however, is incomplete because it excludes political entities. The challenge for an explanatory theory of political economy is how to incorporate political entities into a theory of society. In earlier times when collective activity was less than 10 percent of the totality of economic activity, the pure theory of a market economy could reasonably be viewed as an approximation to a general theory of the social organization of economic activity. The absence of an explanatory theory of collective activity meant the market-based theory was incomplete, but the degree of incompleteness was relatively small.

When collective activity moves into the range of 40 percent or more of economic activity, using the pure theory of markets as an approximation for a theory of the societal whole is surely more questionable. The larger the number of triangles in the lower part of Figure 3 relative to the number of circles, the less will be the probable relevance of a theory based on the presumption that societal observations can be explained as outputs of an open-market process of economic organization. Should the triangles continue to expand relative to the circles, a tipping point will surely be reached where a theory grounded in some version of collectivism will have more explanatory power than one grounded in liberalism.

For instance, consider the treatment of cost within economic theory. Economists define a cost function as a boundary that separates possibility from impossibility. It is always possible to produce above a cost function but never below it. The boundary between possibility and impossibility is defined as conforming to the theoretical proposition that any output is produced by the firm's combining its inputs in a technically efficient manner. There is no way to determine whether firms truly operate in this least-cost manner, not least because it is impossible to say definitively that production at a cost less than what has been observed is possible. It is, however, plausible to think that in the presence of private property, producers will have incentives to choose less costly over more costly means of production because they can bring those differences into their personal accounts. The same institutionally grounded claim cannot be made about political enterprises because there is no enterprise owner who can capture such cost differences. Indeed, a political entity that fails to use its full budgetary appropriation, because its executives determined that they could fulfill their mission without spending all that was appropriated, would almost surely find their budget being reduced the next year.

All entities in society, both private and public, must engage in economic calculation. There is no option to doing so because any choice entails a calculation, which might be implicit and intuitive rather than explicit, but will entail a comparison among options in any case. In any choice between two options, the chooser selects what the chooser regards as the higher valued option (Buchanan 1969). For market enterprises, private property enables the generation of market prices, and those prices provide tools for assisting in economic calculation and securing economic coordination. But how might politically organized enterprises blend into a theory grounded on market organization? The Italian economist Maffeo Pantaleoni (1911) offered some powerful insights into how this might be done. Pantaleoni asked us to imagine a society that contained two bazaars, one that operated with market pricing and the other that operated with political pricing. For Pantaleoni, market pricing was marginal cost pricing, as was consistent with economic theory when he wrote. Within the political bazaar, however, prices charged by the shops in the bazaar were political prices and not market prices.

As an analytical point of departure, unavoidable ambiguity is present when it comes to the specification of political prices. When Pantaleoni wrote, economic theory regarded market prices as being governed by technical conditions of production, which Pantaleoni took to mean marginal cost pricing. In contrast, political prices were not technologically determined because there could be an indefinitely large number of ways an aggregate cost of production could be distributed among taxpayers. To illustrate his theoretical effort, Pantaleoni assumed that political prices were generated by imposing a flat-rate tax on all incomes. Where market prices faced all buyers with the same price under competitive conditions, political prices varied among individuals in proportion to their incomes. Pantaleoni described this pricing scheme as parasitical, not to reflect any normative judgment but to recognize that political prices do not arise through ordinary market transactions. Political enterprises do not have to generate revenue by attracting customers who are free to choose other ways to use their income. To the contrary, political enterprises generate their revenue by making parasitical attachment to market transactions. Political prices are not emergent results of transactions among market participants but are attachments to market transactions that may have little to do with interactions among producers and consumers of political output. A personal income tax, for instance, is an attachment to income-generating transactions in the market, a tax on real estate is an attachment to transactions in real estate, and a retail sales tax is an attachment to those consumer purchases that are included inside the tax base.

What results from this scheme of thought is recognition that political enterprises must use market transactions to gauge values for political activities. Since political enterprises don't engage directly in market transactions, no direct information is generated about the possible value of political activities. The sponsors of political enterprises and programs must look to market enterprises and activities to acquire knowledge about the potential value of different political programs. This parasitical character of political pricing creates an intelligible relationship between private and public enterprises where public enterprises use private enterprises as collectors of information about the potential value of political programs.

Figure 4 gives a simple illustration of what I have in mind. This figure is best thought of as pertaining to enterprise location within some abstract commodity space. Shown there are five clusters of enterprises. Most of those enterprises are shown as circles, some small and some large. There are also several enterprises that resemble circles with needles of irregular length sticking out. For the moment, suppress these entities and look only at the circles. This pattern of enterprise location illustrates the location of enterprises in abstract commodity space as they search for profit. Toward the northwest of Figure 4, relatively many large enterprises are located. The southeast is dominated by small enterprises, while in the center of the enterprise map there are no large enterprises. The point of this exercise is not to set forth some theory of economic location but is rather to illustrate a point about economic calculation and coordination within an environment of political-economic interaction.

Within this framework, market enterprises seek to discover where profitable commercial opportunities reside. To be sure, Figure 4 is a static, frozen representation of what would be better represented as a continual process of some enterprises being created while others are being disbanded. The analytical challenge for an explanatory theory of public finance is to understand where political enterprises locate their activities when they lack the cognitive tools that enable market enterprises to choose where to locate their activities. Following Pantaleoni's insight about parasitical political pricing, a surely reasonable

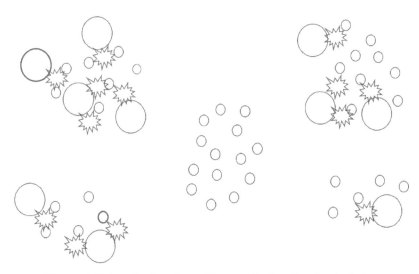

Figure 4 Enterprise location with parasitical political calculation

answer is that the sponsors of political enterprises let the sponsors of market enterprises do the hard leg work for them. Figure 4 illustrates a situation where the middle of the map holds but modest commercial interest, and with the southeast holding only modestly more commercial interest. In contrast, the northwest and northeast are commercially highly attractive.

It is surely a mistaken use of economic theory to think that consumer optimization means that consumers are happy with their situations. They might do the best they can with the options they face, but it is always possible to secure better options under the right institutional arrangement. Within the dyadic relationships of a pure market economy, this is impossible as a reflection of the Pareto efficiency of market equilibrium. For politics, however, the triadic exchanges provide the central template for a theory of social organization through transactions (Podemska-Mikluch and Wagner [2013]). For triadic exchanges, there is typically a majority that gains in part because some of the cost is placed on a minority. The needles emanating from the political entities in Figure 4 illustrate this quality. Political enterprises attach themselves to market enterprises, providing gains beyond what some people could secure through market transactions, with those gains made possible by either taxes or regulatory restrictions placed on other people who thus fare less well under political organization than they would have fared under market organization.

In *Systems of Survival*, Jane Jacobs (1992) explained that a well-working society requires both commercial and guardian modes of activity. Her distinction, moreover, is not the same thing as a distinction between businesses and governments. Even business will engage in guardian activities. While a construction firm will earn its livelihood from its construction activities, it will also engage in some guardian activities. One such activity will entail inventory management and auditing, which are necessary to ensure that employees don't convert company materials to personal use. In reflecting on what happens when commercial and guardian moral syndromes commingle, Jacobs coined the term "monstrous moral hybrids." For instance, an auditor who covers over a theft for a fee is commingling commercial and guardian roles. As businesses become increasingly involved in politics and political enterprises come increasingly to participate in business, monstrous moral hybrids grow within a system of entangled political economy.

The human drama in which we all participate is improvisational and not scripted. There are, however, some time-honored principles that speak to the qualities of various possible dramas. Those principles place commercial and industrial activity in the foreground of the human drama, while putting political action mostly in the background. Over the past century or so, however, foreground and background have become significantly reversed. It is now widely believed that politicians bear primary responsibility for the extent of flourishing within a society. This situation generates a simple but dynamic template that encapsulates the contemporary world. A problem arises. Say an earthquake or fire destroys a good part of a city. In earlier times, recovery would have occurred quickly through the offices of private law. These days, recovery occurs more slowly and fitfully, due to the predominance of public law. With private law you have many businesses seeking opportunities for mutual gain. With public law, you have contending political officials who are using the disaster to project themselves onto society's center stage. There may well be little that politicians can do actively to promote human flourishing other than avoiding the promotion of misery. For instance, a propeller-driven aircraft has natural stability properties. An aircraft that passes through a storm will be tossed up and down, but the plane will continually move toward level flight. Should the pilot react to a dip in the plane's nose by increasing the angle of attack, a stall and possibly a crash can result. Politicians are not pilots of a ship of state, and yet public rhetoric makes them appear to be just that. There is little that politicians can do actively to promote human flourishing other than secure peace, keep taxes low, and administer justice tolerably well. If they stick to this recipe, they will avoid inserting harm into society. That is the best situation any society can attain. All the same, a soberly realistic person would surely be pardoned for thinking that politically induced turbulence will continue to be part of our economic experience, as will the parade of future policy mechanics offering themselves and their programs to control the turbulence their predecessors helped to create.

Vilfredo Pareto (1915 [1935]) distinguished between logical and nonlogical action. Logical action was the domain of market action; nonlogical action was the domain of politics and religion. Pareto's distinction between the two categories of action is not a distinction between rational and irrational action, despite what some commentators have asserted to the contrary. The distinction rather reflects recognition that there are different environments in which people can act, and rational action manifests differently across those environments, much as Gerd Gigerenzer (2008) explains in treating rationality not as a property of a calculating mind but as a product of interaction between mind and environment.

For Pareto, human action was always rational in that action entailed a person's trying to attain a more desirable state of existence, only people face different environments inside of which they act. In this respect, Pareto's concept of action resembled Buchanan's (1969) treatment of the relation between cost and choice. For both Pareto and Buchanan, human action was aimed at achieving a more desired state of existence. How this desire plays out, however, varies with the environment inside of which action occurs. Markets provide one environment; politics provide a different environment. In both environments people face situations where they choose between or among options. And in both environments people seek to do the best they can for themselves. Rational action, however, manifests differently between the environments, as Patrick and Wagner (2015) set forth in their examination of some implications of Pareto's scheme of thought for public choice and political economy.

Market environments face people with situations that resemble scientific experiments, which led Pareto to describe his method as the logico-experimental method. This method pertained equally to people acting as consumers and to people acting as producers. A consumer faces a choice among products and forms a hypothesis or expectation about the satisfaction the different options would yield. To conduct the experiment requires the consumer to pay the price of the product, with the necessity of paying a price leading the consumer to take suitable care in conducting the experiment, much as the economic theory of search later articulated. A producer faces the same setting. In this case, the options might entail different qualities to design into a product or different types of advertising campaigns to conduct. In any such case, the producer forms a hypothesis about the relative value of the different options, and then tests that hypothesis by taking the action and observing the results. Not all experiments are successful, and people are observed on occasion to regret their choices. No one is omniscient, so regret is a feature of life. Still, human action within market environments reflects a substantive form of rationality in human action.

Political environments are different for both voters and politicians. As a purely formal matter, a voter's choice among candidates is identical to a consumer's choice among candidates. In either case, choice requires the chooser to rank the options. With political choice, however, the voter is not actually choosing among the options. To the contrary, the voter is participating in a popularity contest among the candidates. That popularity contest, moreover, revolves around the projection of images (Boulding 1956) and not around the outcome of scientific-like experiments. Competing candidates likewise recognize that they are engaged in popularity contests, so seek to offer projections of images that elicit more favorable responses from voters than the projections of other candidates elicit. Electoral competition is a competitive endeavor just as is market competition. All the same, the environments are different, and those differences lead to the selection of different qualities (Wagner and Yazigi [2014]). As a formal matter, all competitive environments entail rational action aimed at winning the competition. As a substantive matter, environments differ in the amount of genuine deliberation they elicit, with political environments eliciting less deliberation than market environments, as Anthony Downs (1957) recognized in his pioneering effort to put political competition on the same analytical field as market competition, and as Geoffrey Brennan and Loren Lomasky (1993) and Bryan Caplan (2007) recognized in their alternative treatments of rationality in action.

Compare a market setting where a consumer is deciding whether to buy Coca Cola or Pepsi. The choice the buyer makes leads immediately to an outcome, which the buyer can in turn compare against his or her expectation regarding the choice. By contrast, casting a vote does not produce an outcome. That vote has no perceptible impact on the outcome of the election. Furthermore, even if the voter's preferred candidate wins the election, that candidate will not be able to dictate an outcome. Instead, that candidate will become one member inside a complex political process where many possible programs and policies are in play. Voters can always give reasons for supporting one candidate over others, but those reasons will be related to the images different candidates project of themselves as well as to the images a voter might seek to project to friends and acquaintances when engaging in social discussions regarding politics. The voter is still seeking to advance his or her interest when acting in a nonlogical environment, but in no reasonable way can the products of nonlogical action be identified with or assimilated to the products of logical action.

In any field of human activity, it is surely reasonable to surmise that open competition will select for superior qualities in comparison with a competitive arrangement where only a few can enter the competition. Yet political environments differ from market environments, which gives reason to think that the substantive selection of qualities will differ over the forms of competition even though competition as a generic matter selects for excellence among the competitors. For instance, people who are good freestyle swimmers might not be good divers. Nor might excellent divers be swift freestyle swimmers. One would not select a swimming team by watching the candidates dive. Similarly, excellence in commercial competition need not translate into excellence in political competition, though there are areas where the two forms of competition seem to elicit similar qualities. For instance, excellence in commercial advertising entails an ability to create and project images that will resonate with the desires of buyers, creating points of resemblance with political competition. Yet, the buyers who respond to the images the advertisers create are still investing their money in making choices, unlike voters who respond to the images created by political advertisers.

7 Public Debt, Systemic Lying, and the Corruption of Contract

Contracts are promises, as Charles Fried (1981) explains luminously in his treatment of contractual obligation. In this vein, a liberal market economy is a society whose fabric is woven through a dense network of promises and obligations. Contracts entail promises, but promises entail obligations. Hence, a market-based society connects the members of society through the promises they make to one another and the obligations those promises entail.

Societies are not based wholly or even preponderantly on market arrangements, though some market presence will necessarily be present because a truly planned economy without trading and pricing is impossible on a large scale, in contrast to the small-scale tribal societies whose properties Andrew Schmookler (1984) explored. Indeed, much of the twentieth century was dominated by nations where militaristic planning was predominant, with market arrangements being subordinated to military planning, and with Walter Lippmann (1937) exploring how military planning can generate habits of thought and action that promote replacement of liberalism with collectivism as the central default setting for political and social organization. It's not that market arrangements vanish under the predominance of collectivist sentiments and practices. It's rather that those collectivist sentiments become the rules of practical life and not the exception. For instance, learning how to live in the presence of general rationing becomes the norm under generalized military planning, which in turn brings about acquiescence in the many regulatory and administrative offices necessary to operate a system grounded in rationalized military planning. If such planning continues for long, the institutional and behavioral default setting of a society might change from liberalism to collectivism. The liberal default setting is that people can pursue their plans and desires provided they don't violate the similar abilities of other people. In contrast, collectivism morphs into a default setting where people must consult officials and officers to obtain permission across wide swaths of their lives, generating a general deference to politically ensconced holders of power positions.

As a matter of principle, the choice between liberalism and collectivism is clear and stark. Under liberalism, people choose their activities in life and are responsible for their choices. Under collectivism, there are a few people who hold positions of power and who assign the remainder of society to activities the few designate. Collectivism operates under a martial spirit; liberalism operates under a commercial spirit. While the two principles are distinct, there are historical episodes where some blending of those spirits appears to occur. Within societies based on liberalism, military necessity injects a militaristic spirit into society. The militaristic spirit enlists the citizenry into the service of some objectives not of their choosing. If that objective is truly a matter of survival in a brutal and nasty world, that spirit will likely be embraced throughout the land. If the threat to survival is extinguished relatively quickly, the commercial spirit of promise and obligation may quickly resume its centrality to societal life. But should that threat persist, that militaristic spirit may become habitual within a population. Even more, that spirit might be manufactured to marshal support for political programs, along the lines that Coyne and Hall (2018) explain regarding the increasing intrusion of the militaristic spirit into public policing. Indeed, the founders of the American Constitutional Republic worried openly about the need to avoid excessive foreign entanglement because they thought the republican spirit could be eroded through the persistent intrusion of the militaristic spirit into society.

We live in a world that is far removed from any image of a peaceable kingdom where lions lie down with lambs. People may seldom be so innocently engaged as when they are engaging in commerce, as Samuel Johnson averred in the eighteenth century. And it may be difficult to find much public good coming from people who claim to be promoting the public good, as Adam Smith noted in the eighteenth century. And yet well-working societies require both commerce and societal protection, as Jane Jacobs (1992) noted in explaining how survival depends on interaction between commercial and guardian sentiments. Jacobs also noted how "monstrous moral hybrids" might arise if that interaction between the sentiments goes awry, as in the militaristic spirit expanding sufficiently, much as the founders of the American Constitutional Republic recognized.

As an instrument of public finance, taxation is the principal alternative to public debt. So long as governments are financed through balanced budgets, government reflects, though incompletely and imperfectly, the contractual principles of commitment and obligation. The contractual principle is in play because both the option chosen and payment for that option are determined at the same moment under tax finance. To be sure, the contractual principle is only incompletely pursued because tax liabilities are not agreed to by everyone in the Wicksellian fashion. To the contrary, taxes can be imposed in discriminatory fashion to provide advantage to political supporters by imposing loss on political opponents. Still, a government that is financed through a balanced budget is one where the cost of its activities is imposed at the same instant the benefits from its activities manifest in society. A balanced budget reflects the contractual principle in the aggregate, even if it might not do so at the level of individuals.

In contrast, deficit finance violates contractual principles. A budget deficit enables politicians to make commitments to supporters without imposing obligations on opponents, or even on those supporters (Buchanan 1958; Buchanan and Wagner 1977; Salsman 2017). Budget deficits undermine principles of contractual commitment and obligation. Perhaps nowhere is the corruption of contractual principles through public debt so evident as it is with what are described as unfunded liabilities in the United States, which are about five times larger than officially measured public debt ($100 trillion vs. $20 trillion). Unfunded liabilities pertain to programs of what are generally described as social insurance programs. What does it mean to say that unfunded federal liabilities in the United States are around $100 trillion? An unfunded liability reflects the extent to which the political process has generated a set of promises and obligations that cannot be fulfilled, which means in turn that violations of those promises and obligations will necessarily occur in the coming years. Put in its starkest fashion, the existing social insurance programs have made promises to people in their capacities as taxpayers that don't match the promises made to people in their capacities as beneficiaries, and with the promises to beneficiaries exceeding those to taxpayers by something in the vicinity of $100 trillion. When seen through contractual lenses, unfunded liabilities reflect a form of systemic lying, to indicate that the democratic political process as it presently operates promotes such lying as a reasonable strategy of political survival (Bueno de Mesquita et al. 2003).

The systemic lying associated with the various forms of so-called social insurance illustrate how monstrous moral hybrids can arise through a commingling of commercial and guardian syndromes (Jacobs 1992). Insurance arose as a commercial activity that allowed shippers to pool the risks they faced, and that pooling enabled a massive expansion in shipping. The practice of insurance spread from shipping, to insuring against fire losses, to defraying the expenses of hospitalization and disability. By late in the nineteenth century, the commercial principles of insurance had spread throughout the commercial world of private ordering. The organization of insurance under private ordering is a form of contractually based collectivism where the reach of collectivism is limited by the cost of coverage in relation to the willingness of people to buy insurance.

Starting in Europe late in the nineteenth century and coming to the United States early in the twentieth century, governments started to sell social programs under the rubric of "social insurance." Where the purchase of genuine insurance conforms to the principles of logical action, the generation of social insurance fits within Pareto's rubric of nonlogical action. The concept of "insurance" emerged within the commercial setting of private ordering, and the term was well established within public consciousness. People knew what insurance meant, and they appreciated its virtues. The challenge for political salesmanship is always to connect a political program with some positive sentiment that had been previously generated through private ordering. Insurance was such a type of program, and social insurance at the start resembled market-based insurance quite closely, as Carolyn Weaver (1982) explained in her examination of the early history of social security in the United States.

In the first few years following the establishment of the social security program in the United States, the federal government collected taxes but made no payments to beneficiaries. This pattern conformed to the practice of private insurance, and social security was sold originally as following the familiar lines and patterns of private insurance. Within a few years of its creation, however, the social security program was changed to divorce the connection between the payments people made while working and the payments they would receive while retired. After all, what is a politician to do who is sitting on a growing pool of revenue? Rather than operating in genuinely commercial fashion, social security started to operate in a feudal-like manner where the lord of the manor dispensed largesse as he saw fit, only the feudal character of those programs was covered with a veneer of commercial-sounding language to resonate more strongly with popular sentiments that had formed favorable impressions of the market-based insurance that had been gaining momentum over the preceding two centuries. The common mention of some $100 trillion of unfunded liability in federal social insurance programs indicates the divergence between actual practice and the requirements of contractual promising. That gap indicates the divergence between promises made to people in their capacities as recipients and in their capacities as providers of support for those programs. Unfunded liabilities point to systemic lying or corruption.

Debts and credits are promises, and in this there is a problem of the relation between private ordering and public ordering. Long ago, public law received its bearings from private law. Indeed, the central principle of Walter Eucken's (1952) establishment of the Germanic tradition of order theory (*ordnungstheorie*) and its principle of market conformability was that the operation of public law would be rendered congruent with the operation of private law. Such congruence, moreover, was the central feature of Knut Wicksell's suggestions for parliamentary reform in Sweden. Deficit finance corrupts the practice of public promising by leaving implicit the assignment of liabilities for making good on budgetary promises. Public promising becomes corrupted because personal liability for promises has been eliminated from the public square. Even more, liability can be eliminated from the private square as well, as when government credit programs enable otherwise failing firms to continue in business rather than undergoing bankruptcy and reorganization. Public ordering, like private ordering, operates in large extent through exchanges of promises. With private ordering, the question of who promises what to whom generally has a clear answer. With public ordering, however, shifting political coalitions operate to different effect because public ordering creates both voluntary and involuntary debtors. The possessors of those voluntary and involuntary positions, moreover, do not emerge through transactions among freely acting individuals within a framework of logical action. To the contrary, those positions arise and change through the continual effort of ruling political coalitions to provide benefits for supporters by imposing losses on the remainder of society (Riker 1962).

Debtor–creditor relationships involve the making of promises, with those promises continuing in force over some duration of time. The institutional framework of private ordering reinforces the keeping of promises within market-based arrangements. For one thing, people who fail to keep their promises will typically generate bad reputations for themselves, thereby degrading their future commercial opportunities. A good reputation is generally easier to lose than it is to acquire, and the market process generally operates to reward the keeping of promises and punish the failure to keep promises.

Promises operate to different effect within a framework of public ordering than within a system grounded on private ordering. A significant question that often arises with respect to public ordering is just who is promising what to whom? Public entities have no corporate value. Neither do they have any personal locus of responsibility for the value consequences of organizational actions. In the absence of corporate value there is no clear metric for judging corporate performance. Moreover, there is no strong incentive to seek to acquire control of public entities to operate them in a value-enhancing manner. There can be incentives to take over public entities, but not to operate them in a value-enhancing manner because there is no way to acquire a measure of corporate value without transferable ownership. Only in the presence of a market for shares of corporate ownership is it possible to offer informed judgments about the efficiency with which corporate assets are managed. Furthermore, it is the existence of a market for ownership shares that makes it possible to tie executive compensation to future corporate performance through basing a good part of that compensation on stock options rather than salaries. Such forms of executive compensation are impossible for politically held corporations.

It is worth stressing that private ordering creates a form of dyadic exchange while public ordering creates a form of triadic exchange (Podemska-Mikluch and Wagner 2013). Dyadic exchange denotes a relationship of mutual gain among willing participants. While the theory of exchange is commonly illustrated with a simple two-person trade, the theory also covers complex, multi-party commercial interactions, as Richard Epstein (1995) explains in *Simple Rules for a Complex World*. The number of participants is immaterial; it is the voluntary nature of the interaction and participation that is of material interest. By contrast, the triadic exchange organized through public ordering generally entails some people supporting projects they desire by imposing a good part of the cost on unwilling participants in financing those projects. This reflects de Viti de Marco's (1930, 1936) concept of monopolistic democracy.

Suppose that trust is in part a prudential habit that is validated through good experience and undermined through bad experience. Trust might be treated as a type of bathtub theorem. Trust is the level of water in the tub. Good experiences add to the level of the water, while bad experiences subtract water. Within this type of framework, it is easy to understand how private ordering promotes trust. The central institutional framework of private property, freedom of contract, and personal liability channels personal conduct in this manner. Private property incorporates the injunction to avoid taking something that is not yours. Freedom of contract entails recognition that your relationships with other people should be mutually beneficial. Within this institutional framework, the economic world is organized in largely voluntary fashion. For instance, the owner of a business might hire several people to perform various activities. That owner is free to dismiss people who don't perform as they said they would perform. Hence, someone who is not punctual or who is rude to customers or coworkers undermines the value of the firm and can be dismissed. While such dismissal will be costly to the person who was dismissed, it also sets in motion a learning experience, both on the part of the person dismissed and on the part of external observers who also might seek to gain employment. Private ordering will tend to enable the water level in the tub of societal trust to rise.

Public ordering under the principle of consensus or unanimity, as described by de Viti's cooperative state, operates in the same manner. It is different, however, within ordinary democratic frameworks. Politically established relationships have less durability and persistence than market-established relationships. This lowered durability and persistence is a prime operating feature of democratic processes where the composition of coalitions is subject to continual margins of change as currently excluded persons seek to gain political inclusion while currently included persons must be wary of being excluded in the coming days. In this setting, public ordering lowers the level of trust in the societal bathtub relative to private ordering. The simple reason for this is that promises have less durability with public ordering than with private ordering.

Public debt can be approached sensibly only within a theory of political economy and budgeting. It is not sensible to take some measure of public debt as a piece of data and then spin macro theoretic stories about that data. Public debt is not some uncaused cause or primitive variable that can be inserted as an independent variable into some causal chain of analysis. Public debt is one of the outcomes of a budgetary process, with that process residing within some democratic system of political economy. There are an indefinitely large number of systems of democratic political economy, each of which will have its own budgeting system as well as its own arrangements for the generation of public law. In any case, there will always be some cleavage between private and public ordering, with public ordering creating ambiguities where private ordering removes ambiguity. The nature of public ordering is to generate problems that those who administer the affairs of state can wrestle with, expanding in the process the reach of the political into society.

Debts and credits reflect social relationships that continue over some interval of time. Within the framework of private law, credit transactions are governed by the institutional framework of private property and freedom of contract. Contracts are promises that govern future actions, as Charles Fried (1981) explains in his theory of contractual obligation. This framework tends to generate what can be regarded as reasonably well-behaved credit markets. By "well-behaved" I mean that the participants within those markets have clear ideas of what to expect from other participants, and that the entire nexus of market relationships works generally to the mutual advantage of all participants. Within the framework of private law, credit transactions will tend to bring lenders and borrowers together in a way that renders it unlikely that significant opportunities for mutual gain remain unexploited. In this respect, Edward Stringham (2015) shows in his examination of the development of credit markets and institutions that the prime effect of injecting public ordering into credit markets is to restrict the ability of credit markets efficiently to match demanders and suppliers of credit, typically through imposing requirements about transactions that must be made or can't be made.

Public ordering has a strong presence in the operation of credit markets, and that presence potentially can operate in both general and special ways. By "general" I mean the various protective activities associated with the idea that a state's police power can offer help to protect against fraud and other forms of theft. In these activities, political agencies would operate to increase the volume of credit transactions in a general or disinterested manner. By "special" I mean efforts by political agencies to influence how credit is distributed among those who seek credit. For instance, private ordering might provide little or no credit for wind farming because borrowers and lenders cannot locate mutually profitable endeavors by investing in wind farming. Public ordering, however, might generate significant support for wind farming by using the power to tax and the power to monetize public debt to subsidize wind farming.

Such budgetary problems as chronic deficits cannot be reasonably attributed to technical difficulty in budgeting. Sure, modern budgeting is complicated, as it relies on numerous projections about future conditions that are subject unavoidably to error, as Wagner (2012d) examines. Projected tax revenues might exceed what was actually collected for any number of reasons. Expenditures might rise beyond initial projections, as might happen when earthquake damage requires appropriations in excess of what might have been budgeted for such situations. In the face of such unavoidable uncertainty, deficits might arise in some years and surpluses in other years. The greater the uncertainty in making budgetary projections, moreover, the larger the surpluses or deficits will be in individual years. Still, projections are equally likely to overstate as they are to understate the budgetary magnitudes, so there should be no systemic tendency to deficit or surplus over a period of years. Increased technical difficulty in budgeting implies there will be greater variability in the accuracy of budgetary projections, but it does not suggest that systematic deficits will result.

There is surely no option but to conclude that fiscal irresponsibility is a product of political rationality. Stated forthrightly, bad budgeting seems to make for good politics. Furthermore, there are all kinds of collective organizations that manage their budgets well. While budgeting for groups has some added complexity as compared with budgeting for individuals, we have plenty of observations about such groups as corporations, charities, and civic associations managing their budgets well. The only systematic case of budgetary irresponsibility occurs with governmental entities. In light of this simple observation, it becomes necessary to ask what is there about political association that generates a different practical rationality than civil or commercial association? As a formal matter, there is no difference between economic and political rationality. Always, rational action entails replacing less-valued with more-valued options (Buchanan 1969). For there to be divergence between economic and political rationality, people who operate within political settings must face different options than people who operate in commercial or private settings, which they do, as conveyed by Pareto's (1935) distinction between logical and nonlogical action.

With respect to the divergence between economic and political rationality, compare two different ways of organizing transactions in public debt. While all credit transactions bridge time between the initiation of a credit relationship and its extinction, there are different institutional principles by which that bridge can be built. One principle follows private ordering in that the parties to the contract agree to terms at the time the contract is initiated, and subsequent payments are just the completion of what was initially agreed. Transactions in public debt would be handled in the same fashion as personal debt. Suppose a city of one million people borrows $1 billion, or $1,000 per resident. Each of the residents would be assigned liability for $1,000, and that liability would remain with that resident, even entering that person's estate upon death. There can surely be no doubt that this kind of institutional arrangement wherein public law operates in the same way as private law would diminish political support for deficit finance. Where private ordering operates with an explicit exchange of promises, public ordering has a bifurcated quality where some people can impose liabilities on others while concealing their imposition by using the language of contract and promise when there is no such thing in operation with public ordering.

Credit transactions, whether private or public, raise the question, "Who owes what to whom?" For private ordering, what and whom are clear and reside in the contractual relationship the credit transaction establishes. The conventional arrangement for public debt adopts the fiction of collective liability for public debt, as expressed by the oft-asserted claim that "we owe it to ourselves." From this ideological assertion, it is a short step for a supporter of debt-financed spending to claim that the discharge of this collective liability is the province of those who operate the political process. The normal outcome of such democratic processes is that many people become forced debtors, in that they would rather have had less debt and less expenditure but were dominated by an alternative political coalition (Eusepi and Wagner 2017). An alternative arrangement where liabilities to service public debt are made explicit at the time of political decision establishes relationships of promise and obligation. This alternative institutional setting of budget balance mirrors private credit transactions, in that people are assigned shares of liability for collective actions that create public debt.

Recognition that political rationality can promote fiscal irresponsibility has led to promotion of numerous possible institutional remedies, going back at least to sinking funds in the 1700s. In contemporary times, proposals to require budget balance have been in the forefront of suggestions for securing a greater measure of fiscal control and responsibility. In his examination of how rules might restrain budgetary excesses, David Primo (2007) explains that federal legislation was enacted in the United States in 1979 to require a balanced budget starting in 1982. That legislation, known as Byrd-Grassley, has not been repealed and so remains on the books. Aside from surpluses in 1999 and 2000, however, deficits have remained the normal pattern of democratic business. All American states except one also require the avoidance of budget deficits, and yet most states operate with budget deficits. James Miller (1994) subtitled his memoir on his experience as director of the Office of Management and Budget under President Reagan as "Urgings of an Abominable No-Man." While Miller generally favored smaller government, we may be sure that his urgings while acting as budget director removed but a proverbial drop in the bucket of governmental red ink.

The tide of red ink could not be held back by rules that did not reflect widespread sentiment, as Friedrich Wieser (1926) and Bertrand de Jouvenel (1948) recognized in treating power within democratic polities as more a matter of massed sentiment than of martial force. Those sentiments surely reflect a century of semipermanent warfare in the Western world that began early in the twentieth century, and subsequently have been extended, even if hyperbolically, to such things as wars on poverty, drugs, illiteracy, and so on. Popular (democratic) government is ruled by sentiment, with governing elites competing with one another to get in front of such sentiment. We may doubt, though, that sentiment is autonomous. More likely, sentiment derives at least in part from practice. And practice has not been disciplined by budget balance for nearly a century. If contemporary massed sentiments were captured by Adam Smith's expression of good government, it is surely reasonable to think that Byrd-Grassley would have been implemented, Miller's abominable urgings would have taken hold, and states would not be heavily indebted. Absent Smith-like sentiments exercising a deep hold over the mores resident within the population, formal rules will be more on the order of annoyances than instruments for changing conduct.

The letter of a rule can be obeyed even as the spirit of the rule is violated. This will surely happen to the extent that the imposition of a rule is generally regarded as an outcome of faction and not a genuine reflection of good government. In such situations, the letter of the law can remain on the books while the spirit of the law is bypassed by playing upon ambiguity that is a feature of nearly all efforts to create formal rules. To declare that a government is to operate within a balanced budget rule is not a point of destination, but is only a starting point, so long as there is no consensus regarding the rightness of the rule. A balanced budget might be enacted to start a year, but revenues might fall short of what had been expected. Alternatively, some natural catastrophe might occur, with strong legislative support coalescing around borrowing to finance a supplemental appropriation.

Even more, budgetary categories and magnitudes aren't objectively given conditions, but are defined through political choice. For instance, many federal programs in the United States are defined as being uncontrollable because they are subject to legislated formulas. But these formulas could always be changed, and sometimes they are, only legislators mostly prefer to avoid getting embroiled in such matters and so assert the category of uncontrollable expenditures. These expenditures are uncontrollable as a matter of political convention, but they are not uncontrollable in the sense that the elevation of Mount Everest is uncontrollable. There can be political programs that operate according to a formula where no legislative support exists for changing the formula. These magnitudes are uncontrollable within a particular political apparatus that represents life on the fiscal commons.

Not all governmental activity, moreover, appears on a budget. Activities that appear on a budget in one year can be moved onto off-budget status, evading budget limits in the process. Government-sponsored enterprises don't appear on government budgets. For instance, a state highway department can reduce its budget by transferring its spending for snow removal to a turnpike authority that operates as a government-sponsored enterprise. Even more, regulation is always a possible substitute for budgeting. A city that finances snow removal on city streets can require homeowners to remove the snow from subdivision streets adjacent to their homes, just as they are now required to remove snow from sidewalks. Without doubt, better rules can help, but they won't denote the end of history and the use of political power to secure ends the holders of such power desire. Rules don't act directly on actions because they must be filtered through beliefs that are present within a population. In short, formal rules won't overcome opposition based on tacit recognition that the rules are more vehicles of factional interest than reflections of public interest.

8 From Liberal to Feudal Democracy: Henry Maine Reversed

This monograph is centered on the theme that societies are continually evolving through interaction among an ever-changing cast of members who do *not* share some universal hard core of common belief that would render disagreements of second-order significance. To be sure, economic theory typically presumes that a core exists for an economic system, which it probably does under private ordering (Telser 1994). Under public ordering where the agenda of collective action is dominated by redistributions of wealth and by conferrals of privileges at the expense of other people, cores will typically be absent. This doesn't mean collectivities won't be able to act, but rather means that observed action will be arbitrary expressions of the power to control political agenda, as Romer and Rosenthal (1978) and Shepsle and Weingast (1981) explain. In the absence of a core, societies will feature continuing contestation over position and status. This contestation will generate evolutionary movement through time. The United States began as what can reasonably be described as a system of liberal democracy. The liberal orientation held that people were responsible for conducting their lives within the institutional framework provided by private property and freedom of contract, with some modest accommodation made for a small amount of political action. Within this framework, social organization emerged largely through free markets, as modified by modest government action. Such government action as there was, moreover, was carried out mostly by state and local governments and not by the federal government, as Jonathan Hughes (1977) explained in *The Governmental Habit*, which explored governmentally imposed economic controls in colonial America.

The liberal republicanism of early America contrasted with the feudal arrangements that dominated Europe at the time. Feudal arrangements were hierarchical and were arrangements into which people were born. If well bred, you would be a lord who had some contribution to make to governance of the realm. If you were not well bred, you would tend to your station in life and not concern yourself with what was not yours to be concerned about. In contrast to these feudal arrangements, the American Declaration of Independence asserted that "governments derive their just powers from the consent of the governed." In contrast to the feudal pattern of a multiplicity of intersecting duties and obligations, liberal republicanism began with individual liberty, with governments deriving their just powers from consent among the people to be governed. Writing in the mid-nineteenth century, Henry Maine (1861) summarized the pattern of social evolution up to that point by declaring that "the direction of movement of the progressive societies has been one from status to contract." Contract is the realm of private ordering; status is the realm of public ordering.

Over the past century or so throughout the west, however, this direction of societal movement has reversed. This ongoing transformation from contract back to status that has been underway for a good century is a product of the search for support within a democratic polity, as Randall Holcombe (2002) explains. It should not be thought that this transformation reflects some move from inferior to superior, as is often thought to be the outcome of competitive processes. This might be a reasonable conclusion to reach in environments that are driven by logical action. This quality doesn't follow, however, for environments driven by the sentimentality of nonlogical action. With respect to sentimentality, it is often thought, following Adam Smith (1759), that sentiment works for the public good through approbation. There are certainly circumstances where this is possible, but this is surely not a universal possibility.

Approbation entails creating rank orders with respect to relative deservedness. As Arthur Lovejoy (1936) explains, approbation is cousin to envy, which Helmut Schoeck (1969) explores as a basis for social theory. If everyone in society possessed the same scale of valuation, approbation would work as Smith claimed. But if those scales differ among people, what is approbation for some can become envy for others. Is commercial success an object of worthiness that elicits approbation? Within some precincts of society, it surely is. But there are surely other precincts where commercial success is not an object of worthiness, and where it elicits envy instead. At this point we enter some treacherous territory regarding the relationship between private and public ordering and the place of sentiment within an environment of nonlogical action.

Can private ordering maintain itself, or might it degenerate into public ordering? Consider a simple model where five new businesses are established, two of which succeed and three of which fail. If the three enterprises that failed come to admire the qualities of those enterprises that succeeded, perhaps approbation would operate to reinforce private ordering throughout the society. But what if those who fail invoke some claim that those who succeeded operated with some unfair advantage, however that might be construed? Perhaps those who failed claimed they were disadvantaged by entering commercial life with less useful personal connections and experience. Might not people in this position possibly be susceptible to expanded public ordering through democratic competition for office wherein candidates offer to create programs to address such situations? And might not public ordering operate as a self-fulfilling prophecy because the resulting creation of entitlements for those who failed promote yet further failure, further increasing the demand for entitlement through public ordering?

In *Capitalism, Socialism, and Democracy*, Joseph Schumpeter (1944) argued that capitalism or liberalism was destined to give way to socialism or collectivism. Schumpeter seems to have been right with respect to the general direction of movement within societies since late in the nineteenth century, with one possible caveat. Politics and public ordering are responsive and reactive, they are rarely creative. It is difficult to see how creative action could originate in politics, at least within democratic regimes where some modicum of agreement is necessary for action to take place. So, we have a process illustrated by Figure 4, where entrepreneurs locate profit opportunities, and then political operators move in to claim some of the low-hanging fruit, so to speak.

Within this setting, there is always a form of cat-and-mouse game in play. Entrepreneurs locate sources of wealth, and after some period of operation politicians identify those entrepreneurs and their activities. Thereafter, entrepreneurs must operate differently because they are inside the shadow of the state. While this is happening, however, new entrepreneurs are identifying new opportunities outside the state's shadow. Entrepreneurial gains are thus short-lived and not permanent. But how much does this short-lived character really matter? Perhaps economists have exaggerated the significance of permanence due to their fascination with equilibrium models, which are always reducible to present values and permanent relationships. At a 10 percent rate of discount, however, a rent that lasts seven years is about half as valuable as one that lasts forever, and half of forever is quite a long time. Perhaps our equilibrium theories have blinded us to the significance of temporary rents in the organization of human affairs.

9 Liberalism and Collectivism: An Easily Toxic Mix

Political philosophies are abstract representations of a more complex world of practice. Liberalism and collectivism are abstract nouns that are theoretical representations of a reality that is more complex than any philosophy can capture. It is for this reason that I have described liberalism and collectivism as default settings, as distinct from their providing concrete guides to the world of practice. A default setting is a point of departure for providing orientation regarding concrete practice. Liberalism is a default setting that maintains that individuals bear ultimate responsibility for their conduct and the biographies they construct as they live their lives. In contrast, collectivism entails a default setting that holds that the quality of living a good life is a collective and not an individual responsibility. In exploring the liberal–collective polarity, we must take care to avoid letting formal abstractions replace recognition that living is more a substantive than a formal matter. Sure, we can't live on bread alone. We also need ideas to live by; moreover, ideas speak to the form from which substance is derived.

Living well requires some ability to navigate between form and substance, and that intermediate territory is populated by the organizations and practices of what is often denoted as civil society (Alexander 2006), which is neither market nor state and yet can be corrupted from either direction. One direction strips people of ordinary sympathies for other people; the other direction reduces those sympathies to ordinary political action. These days, the intrusion of the political into the precincts of civil society seems the greater danger to a good social order. Ideas do matter. Keynes was right on this account, even though he was wrong on macroeconomics. Economic theory has labored for a century or more under the ideological construction of an autonomous individual with given preferences, and with societies being arenas where people satisfy their preferences. This construction was set forth lucidly by George Stigler and Gary Becker (1977), and Ross Emmett (2006) set forth the infirmities of that construction in conjecturing what Frank Knight would have said about the Stigler–Becker construction. For Stigler and Becker, economic theory was reducible to individual optimization within a market context. For Knight, by contrast, economics offered a point of entry into a science of society, only society is not the same kind of object as the individuals who constitute a society.

Norbert Elias (1939a, 1939b) recognized fruitfully the challenges that arose in bridging the gap between individual action and the societal environment in which everyone must operate. While it is good for economists to be concerned about the micro foundations of their theories of a macro system, there is also much work to be done on the systems foundations for individual action. Liberalism in this respect is not a theory of rational individual action that is developed by extracting individuals and their concerns from the societal contexts inside of which they operate. Liberalism follows Knight's path more than the Stigler–Becker path, with respect to the option Ross Emmett (2006) described. Liberalism is the realm of the private ordering of human activity, where private ordering pertains to some social process of discussion, deliberation, and adjudication. Its default setting is that people are free to determine their actions, provided only that they don't impair the similar abilities of other people. For instance, a person would be free to establish a business of his or her choice without having to secure permission from political authorities. To be sure, a successful business will require participation from many people, all of whom act within the liberal framework of private ordering. To establish a new business, the person will need to find a place of business. This must be accomplished through voluntary agreement. The new business will need to recruit a work force. Again, this will have to be accomplished through voluntary agreement. And finally, the business will need to attract customers in sufficient volume to make the business a going concern.

Absent from this world of private ordering is political compulsion, which is different from authority and leadership inside society along the lines that Ion

Sterpan and Richard Wagner (2017) stressed in distinguishing leadership from politically manifested power. The owner of a new business will not be able to call upon support from tax-financed political entities because taxes are forcible extractions from taxpayers and not voluntary contributions offered by investors. The political philosophy of liberalism yields an abstract representation of the world of practice that is organized through voluntary transactions within the common law principles of property, contract, and liability, along the lines that Walter Eucken (1952) explained in setting forth a theory of public policy that is consonant with the political philosophy of liberalism. The political philosophy of liberalism has as its default setting acceptance of the responsibility of people for their own actions. This doesn't mean that people invariably get what they want in life because they must operate inside the private law principles of property, contract, and liability. It means only that there is no autonomous source of power that can prevent people from undertaking desired actions or can force people to take undesired actions. The *modus operandi* of private ordering is discussion and consent.

In contrast, the political philosophy of collectivism, of which there are many versions, has at its core a two-level division of society into governors and governed. All collectivisms envision some yoking of people together to advance some common purpose. Understandably, collectivist notions come readily into the foreground in times of war, under the reasonable notion that people mostly place high value on their survival. The political philosophy of collectivism must operate with a scheme where the few govern the many. To be sure, the various versions of collectivism all hold that the few will govern for the benefit of the many. Even the large-scale butchers of the twentieth century claimed that they sought to do good in the world. No one ever claims to want power to wreak evil on the world. And yet concentrated power often works this way. With collectivism as a default setting, people must assume that along various margins of action they will require consent and consultation with holders of political office. Within a nation, a president or prime minister would be regarded as the CEO of the nation, as distinct from being merely the CEO of a set of political entities inside a nation where the society is far more extensive than the reach of a national government.

It is a vicious category mistake of monumental proportions to assert that democratic states can be indebted, even though it was fully reasonable to recognize that monarchs could become indebted. It is a category mistake because it misconstrues the problem of achieving good democratic governance as one of selecting the right preference ordering to impose on society, and with elections being the method for selecting that ordering. That category mistake is particularly vicious because it promotes collectivist public sentiments that undermine the virtues of sobriety and rectitude that are vital for self-governing republics along the lines that Vincent Ostrom (1997) dissects in his examination of the challenge Alexis de Tocqueville posed regarding the problematic of maintaining self-governing republics.

References

Alexander, J. C. (2006). *The Civil Sphere*. Oxford: Oxford University Press.

Arrow, K. J. (1951). *Social Choice and Individual Values*. New York: John Wiley.

Backhaus, J. G. and Wagner, R. E. (1987). The Cameralists: A public choice perspective. *Public Choice* 53: 3–20.

Backhause, R. E. and Medema, S. G. (2012). Economists and the analysis of government failure: fallacies in the interpretations of Cambridge welfare economics. *Cambridge Journal of Economics* 36: 981–94.

Barro, R. J. (1974). Are government bonds net wealth? *Journal of Political Economy* 82: 1095–1118.

Black, D. (1958). *The Theory of Committees and Elections*. Cambridge: Cambridge University Press.

Blaug, M. (1996). *Economic Theory in Retrospect*, 5th ed. Cambridge: Cambridge University Press.

Boettke, P. J. (2001). *Calculation and Coordination*. London: Routledge.

Boettke, P. J. (2007). Liberty vs. power in economic policy in the 20th and 21st centuries. *Journal of Private Enterprise* 22: 7–36.

Boettke, P. J. (2018). *F. A. Hayek: Economics, Political Economy, and Social Philosophy*. London: Palgrave Macmillan.

Boulding, K. E. (1956). *The Image: Knowledge in Life and Society*. Ann Arbor: University of Michigan Press.

Brennan, G. and Lomasky, L. (1993). *Democracy and Decision: The Pure Theory of Electoral Preference*. Cambridge: Cambridge University Press.

Brubaker, E. R. (1997). The tragedy of the public budgetary commons. *The Independent Review* 1: 353–70.

Buchanan, J. M. (1949). The pure theory of public finance: a suggested approach. *Journal of Political Economy* 57: 496–505.

Buchanan, J. M. (1958). *Public Principles of Public Debt*. Homewood, IL: Richard D. Irwin.

Buchanan, J. M. (1960). The Italian tradition in fiscal theory. In J. M. Buchanan, ed., *Fiscal Theory and Political Economy*. Chapel Hill: University of North Carolina Press, pp. 24–74.

Buchanan, J. M. (1967). *Public Finance in Democratic Process*. Chapel Hill: University of North Carolina Press.

Buchanan, J. M. (1968). *The Demand and Supply of Public Goods*. Chicago: Rand McNally.

Buchanan, J. M. (1969). *Cost and Choice*. Chicago: Markham.

Buchanan, J. M. and Tullock, G. (1962). *The Calculus of Consent*. Ann Arbor: University of Michigan Press.

Buchanan, J. M. and Wagner, R. E. (1977). *Democracy in Deficit: The Political Legacy of Lord Keynes*. New York: Academic Press.

Bueno de Mesquita, B., Smith, A., Siverson, R. M., et al. 2003. *The Logic of Political Survival*. Cambridge, MA: MIT Press.

Bulow, J. and Rogoff, K. (1988). Sovereign debt: is to forgive to forget? *American Economic Review* 79: 43–50.

Bulow, J. and Rogoff, K. (1989). A constant recontracting model of sovereign debt. *Journal of Political Economy* 97: 155–78.

Calvo, G. (1988). Servicing public debt: the role of expectations. *American Economic Review* 78: 647–61.

Caplan, B. (2007). *The Myth of the Rational Voter*. Princeton: Princeton University Press.

Congleton, R. D. (2011). *Perfecting Parliament: Constitutional Reform, Liberalism, and the Rise of Western Democracy*. Cambridge: Cambridge University Press.

Coyne, C. and Hall, A. (2018). *Tyranny Comes Home: The Domestic Fate of U.S. Militarism*. Stanford, CA: Stanford University Press.

Cruces, J. and Trebesch, C. (2013). Sovereign defaults: the price of haircuts. *American Economic Journal: Macroeconomics* 5: 85–117.

De Jouvenel, B. (1993 [1948]). *On Power: The Natural History of its Growth*. Indianapolis: Liberty Fund.

De Jouvenel, B. (1961). The chairman's problem. *American Political Science Review* 55: 368–72.

De Viti de Marco, A. (1888). *Il carattere teorico dell'economia finanziaria*. Rome: Pasqualucci.

De Viti de Marco, A. (1930). *Un trentennio di lotte politiche*. Roma: Collezione Meridionale Editrice.

De Viti de Marco, A. (1936). *First Principles of Public Finance*. London: Jonathan Cape.

Downs, A. (1957). *An Economic Theory of Democracy*. New York: Harper & Row.

Edgeworth, F. Y. (1897). The pure theory of taxation. *Economic Journal* 7: 100–22.

Elias, N. (1982 [1939a]). *The Civilizing Process*. New York: Pantheon Books.

Elias, N. (1991 [1939b]). *The Society of Individuals*. Oxford: Basil Blackwell.

Emmett, R. N. (2006). De gustibus est disputandum: Frank H. Knight's response to George Stigler and Gary Becker's "De gustibus non est disputandum." *Journal of Economic Methodology* 13: 97–111.

Epstein, R. A. 1995. *Simple Rules for a Complex World*. Cambridge, MA: Harvard University Press.

Eucken, W. (1952). *Grundsätze der Wirtschaftspolitik*. Tübingen: Mohr Siebeck.

Eusepi, G. and Wagner, R. E. (2013). Tax prices in a democratic polity: The continuing relevance of Antonio de Viti de Marco. *History of Political Economy* 45: 99–121.

Eusepi, G. and Wagner, R. E. (2017). *Public Debt: An Illusion of Democratic Political Economy*. Cheltenham, UK: Edward Elgar.

Fried, C. (1981). *Contract as Promise: A Theory of Contractual Obligation*. Cambridge, MA: Harvard University Press.

Garrison, R. (2001). *Time and Money: The Macroeconomics of Capital Structure*. London: Routledge.

Gigerenzer, G. 2008. *Rationality for Mortals*. Oxford: Oxford University Press.

Goldscheid, R. 1917. *Staatssozialismus oder Staatskapitalismus*. Vienna: Brüder Suschitzky.

Greve, M. (2012). *The Upside-Down Constitution*. Cambridge, MA: Harvard University Press.

Grossman, H. and Van Huyck, J. (1988). Sovereign debt as a contingent claim: excusable default, repudiation, and reputation. *American Economic Review* 78: 1088–97.

Harrod, R. (1951). *The Life of John Maynard Keynes*. London: Macmillan.

Hayek, F. A. (1932). *Monetary Policy and the Trade Cycle*. London: Jonathan Capel.

Hayek, F. A. (1935). *Prices and Production*, 2nd ed. London: Routledge and Kegan Paul.

Hayek, F. A. (1937). Economics and knowledge. *Economica* 4: 33–54.

Hayek, F. A. (1945). The use of knowledge in society. *American Economic Review* 35: 519–30.

Hickel, R., ed. 1976. *Die Finanzkrise der Steuerstaats*. Frankfurt: Suhrkamp.

Higgs, R. (1997). Regime uncertainty: why the Great Depression lasted so long and why prosperity resumed after the war. *The Independent Review* 1: 561–90.

Holcombe, R. G. (2002). *From Liberty to Democracy: The Transformation of American Government*. Ann Arbor: University of Michigan Press.

Hughes, J. R. T. (1977). *The Governmental Habit*. New York: Basic Books.

Jacobs, J. (1992). *Systems of Survival*. New York: Random House.

Justi, J. H. G. (1771 [1969]). *Natur und Wesen der Staaten*. Darmstadt: Scientia Verlag Aalen.

Keynes, J. M. 1936. *The General Theory of Employment, Interest, and Money*. New York: Harcourt Brace.

Koppl, R. (2002). *Big Players and the Economic Theory of Expectations*. New York: Palgrave Macmillan.

Koppl, R. (2018). *Expert Failure*. Cambridge: Cambridge University Press.

Lachmann, L. (1977). *Capital, Expectations, and the Market Process*. Kansas City: Sheed, Andrews and McMeel.

Levine, M. E. and Plott, C. R. 1977. Agenda influence and its implications. *Virginia Law Review* 63: 561–604.

Lewis, P. A. and Wagner, R. E. (2017). New Austrian macro theory: a call for inquiry. *Review of Austrian Economics* 30: 1–18.

Lindahl, E. (1958 [1919]). Just taxation: a positive solution. In R. A. Musgrave and A. T. Peacock, eds., *Classics in the Theory of Public Finance*. London: Macmillan, pp. 168–76.

Lippmann, W. (1922). *Public Opinion*. New York: Harcourt Brace.

Lippmann, W. (1937). *The Good Society*. Boston: Little, Brown.

Lovejoy. A. O. 1936. *The Great Chain of Being*. Cambridge, MA: Harvard University Press.

Machlup, F. 1935. The consumption of capital in Austria. *Review of Economics and Statistics* 17: 13–19.

Maine, H. (1861). *Ancient Law*. London: John Murray.

Martinez-Vasquez, J. and Winer, S. L., eds. (2014). *Coercion and Social Welfare in Public Finance*. Cambridge: Cambridge University Press.

May, J. D. (1965). Democracy, organization, and Michels. *American Political Science Review* 59: 417–29.

McLure, M. (2007). *The Paretian School and Italian Fiscal Sociology*. Basingstoke: Palgrave Macmillan.

Medema, S. G. (1996). Of Pangloss, Pigouvians, and pragmatism: Ronald Coase and social cost analysis. *Journal of the History of Economic Thought* 18: 96–114.

Michels, R. (1915 [1962]). *Political Parties: A Sociological Study of the Oligarchic Tendencies of Modern Democracy*. New York: Collier Books.

Miller, J. C. III. 1994. *Fix the US Budget! Urgings of an Abominable No-Man*. Stanford, CA: Hoover Institution Press.

Mirrlees, J. A. 1994. Optimal taxation and government finance. In J. M. Quigley and E. Smolensky, eds. *Modern Public Finance*. Cambridge, MA: Harvard University Press, pp. 213–31.

Mosca, M. 2016. *Antonio de Viti de Marco: a story worth remembering*. Basingstoke, UK: Palgrave Macmillan.

Musgrave, R. A. (1939). The voluntary exchange theory of public economy. *Quarterly Journal of Economics* 53: 213–37.

Odom, J. (2019). *Public Debt and the Common Good: Philosophical and Institutional Implications of Fiscal Imbalance.* London: Routledge.

O'Driscoll, G. (1977). *Economics as a Coordination Problem.* Kansas City: Sheed, Andrews and McMeel.

Ostrom, E. (1990). *Governing the Commons.* Cambridge: Cambridge University Press.

Ostrom, V. (1987). *The Political Theory of a Compound Republic*, 2nd ed. Lincoln: University of Nebraska Press.

Ostrom, V. (1997). *The Meaning of Democracy and the Vulnerability of Democracies: A Response to Tocqueville's Challenge.* Ann Arbor: University of Michigan Press.

Pantaleoni, M. (1911). Considerazioni dulle proprieta di un sistema di prezzi politici. *Giornale degli Economisti* 42: 9–29, 114–33.

Pareto, V. (1915 [1935]). *The Mind and Society.* New York: Harcourt Brace.

Patrick, M. and Wagner, R. E. (2015). From mixed economy to entangled political economy: a Paretian social-theoretic orientation. *Public Choice* 164: 103–16.

Pigou, A. C. (1920). *The Economics of Welfare.* London: Macmillan.

Pigou, A. C. (1928). *A Study in Public Finance.* London: Macmillan.

Plott, C. R. and Levine, M. E. (1978). A model of agenda influence on committee decisions. *American Economic Review* 68: 146–60.

Podemska-Mikluch, M. and Wagner, R. E. 2013. Dyads, triads, and the theory of exchange. *Review of Austrian Economics* 26: 171–82.

Polanyi, M. 1958. *Personal Knowledge.* Chicago: University of Chicago Press.

Primo, D. 2007. *Rules and Restraint: Government Spending and the Design of Institutions.* Chicago: University of Chicago Press.

Puviani, A. (1903). *Teoria della illusion finanziaria.* Palermo: Sandron.

Puviani, A. (1960). *Die Illusionen in der öffentlichen Finanzwirtschaft.* Translated by M. Hartmann and F. Rexhausen. Berlin: Duncker and Humblot.

Ramsey, F. P. (1927). A contribution to the theory of taxation. *Economic Journal* 37: 47–61.

Raudla, R. (2010). Governing the budgetary commons: what can we learn from Elinor Ostrom? *European Journal of Law and Economics* 30: 201–21.

Resnick, M. (1994). *Turtles, Termites, and Traffic Jams.* Cambridge, MA: MIT Press.

Riker, W. (1962). *The Theory of Political Coalitions.* New Haven, CT: Yale University Press.

Romer, T. and Rosenthal, H. (1978). Political resource allocation, controlled agenda, and the status quo. *Public Choice* 33: 27–43.

Rothschild, K. 1996. Keynes's *General Theory*: a look at the criss-cross of reviews. *Journal of Post-Keynesian Economics* 18: 533–45.

Salsman, R. M. (2017). *The Political Economy of Public Debt*. Cheltenham, UK: Edward Elgar.

Samuelson, P. A. (1954). The pure theory of public expenditure. *The Review of Economics and Statistics* 36: 387–89.

Samuelson, P. A. (1955). Diagrammatic exposition of a theory of public expenditure. *Review of Economics and Statistics* 37: 350–56.

Schmölders, G. (1959). Fiscal psychology: a new branch of public finance. *National Tax Journal* 12: 340–45.

Schmölders, G. (1960). *Das Irrationale in der öffentlichen Finanzwirtschaft: Probleme der Finanzpsychologie*. Hamburg: Rowahlt.

Schmookler, A. B. (1984). *The Parable of the Tribes: The Problem of Power in Social Evolution*. Albany: State University of New York Press.

Schoeck, H. (1969). *Envy: A Theory of Social Behavior*. New York: Van Nostrand.

Schumpeter, J. A. (1954 [1918]). The crisis of the tax state. *International Economic Papers* 4: 5–38. Reprinted in Hickel (1976).

Schumpeter, J. A. (1944). *Capitalism, Socialism, and Democracy*. New York: Harper & Row.

Seater, J. J. (1993). Ricardian equivalence. *Journal of Economic Literature* 31: 142–90.

Shackle, G. L. S. (1968). Uncertainty in Economics and Other Essays. Cambridge: Cambridge University Press.

Shackle, G. L. S. (1972). *Epistemics and Economics*. Cambridge: Cambridge University Press.

Shepsle, K. A. and Weingast, B. R. (1981). Structure induced equilibrium and legislative choice. *Public Choice* 37: 503–19.

Smith, A. (1976 [1759]). *The Theory of Moral Sentiments*. Indianapolis: Liberty Fund.

Smith, A. (1937 [1776]). *An Inquiry into the Nature and Causes of the Wealth of Nations*. New York: Modern Library.

Sterpan, I. and Wagner, R. E. (2017). The autonomy of the political in political economy. *Advances in Austrian Economics* 22: 133–57.

Stigler, G. J. and Becker, G. S. (1977). De gustibus non est disputandum. *American Economic Review* 67: 76–90.

Stringham, E. (2015). *Private Governance*. Oxford: Oxford University Press.

Telser, L. (1994). The usefulness of core theory in economics. *Journal of Economic Perspectives* 8: 151–64.

Tomz, M. (2007). *Reputation and International Cooperation: Sovereign Debt across Three Centuries*. Princeton: Princeton University Press.

Tribe, K. (1984). Cameralism and the science of government. *Journal of Modern History* 56: 263–84.

Veetil, V. and Wagner, R. E. (2018). Nominal GDP stabilization: chasing a mirage. *Quarterly Review of Economics and Finance* 67: 227–36.

Wagner, R. E. (1986). Liability rules, fiscal institutions, and the debt. In C. K. Rowley and R. D. Tollison, eds. *Deficits*. Oxford: Oxford University Press, pp. 374–90.

Wagner, R. E. (1988). *The Calculus of Consent*: a Wicksellian retrospective. *Public Choice* 56: 153–66.

Wagner, R. E. (1992). Grazing the federal budgetary commons: the rational politics of budgetary irresponsibility. *Journal of Law and Politics* 9: 105–19.

Wagner, R. E. (2007). *Fiscal Sociology and the Theory of Public Finance*. Cheltenham, UK: Edward Elgar.

Wagner, R. E. (2012a). The Cameralists: fertile sources for a new science of public finance. In J. G. Backhaus, ed., *Handbook of the History of Economic Thought*. New York: Springer, pp. 123–35.

Wagner, R. E. (2012b). A macro economy as an ecology of plans. *Journal of Economic Behavior and Organization* 82: 433–44.

Wagner, R. E. (2012c). Viennese kaleidics: why it's liberty more than policy that calms turbulence. R*eview of Austrian Economics* 25: 283–97.

Wagner, R. E. (2012d). *Deficits, Debt, and Democracy: Wrestling with Tragedy on the Fiscal Commons*. Cheltenham, UK: Edward Elgar.

Wagner, R. E. (2016). *Politics as a Peculiar Business: Insights from a Theory of Entangled Political Economy*. Cheltenham, UK: Edward Elgar.

Wagner, R. E. (2017a). *James M. Buchanan and Liberal Political Economy: A Rational Reconstruction*. Lanham, MD: Lexington Books.

Wagner, R. E. (2017b). *Public Debt and the Corruption of Contract*; published simultaneously as *Il debito pubblico e la corruzione delle promesee*. Milan: Bruno Leoni Institute.

Wagner, R. E. and Yazigi, D. (2014). Form vs. substance in selection through competition: elections, markets, and political economy. *Public Choice* 159: 503–14.

Weaver, C. L. 1982. *The Crisis in Social Security: Economic and Political Origins*. Durham, NC: Duke University Press.

Wicksell, K. (1896). *Finanztheoretische Untersuchungen*. Jena: Gustav Fischer.

Wicksell, K. (1958). A new principle of just taxation. In R. A. Musgrave and A. T. Peacock, eds., *Classics in the Theory of Public Finance*. London: Macmillan, pp. 72–118.

Wieser, F. (1926). *Das Gesetz der Macht*. Vienna: Julius Springer.

Witt, U. (1997). The Hayekian puzzle: spontaneous order and the business cycle. *Scottish Journal of Political Economy* 44: 44–58.

Acknowledgments

I am grateful to Peter J. Boettke and an anonymous reviewer for helpful comments and suggestions on an earlier version of this Element.

Austrian Economics

Peter Boettke
George Mason University

Peter Boettke is a Professor of Economics & Philosophy at George Mason University, the BB&T Professor for the Study of Capitalism, and the director of the F. A. Hayek Program for Advanced Study in Philosophy, Politics and Economics at the Mercatus Center at George Mason University.

About the Series

This series will primarily be focused on contemporary developments in the Austrian School of Economics and its relevance to the methodological and analytical debates at the frontier of social science and humanities research, and the continuing relevance of the Austrian School of Economics for the practical affairs of public policy throughout the world.

Cambridge Elements ☰

Austrian Economics

CPSIA information can be obtained
at www.ICGtesting.com
Printed in the USA
LVHW011732210519
618624LV00015B/359/P

9 781108 735896